DARK KNIGHTS 2

The Dark Humor of Police Officers

Border Patrol Edition

By

Robert L. Bryan

Dark Knights 2 – Border Patrol Edition

By Robert L. Bryan

Copyright 2018 by Robert L. Bryan

From the Author

Thank you for purchasing DARK KNIGHTS 2 – BORDER PATROL EDITION. This book is a prequel to DARK KNIGHTS – THE DARK HUMOR OF POLICE OFFICERS. The first Dark Knights chronicles the timeline of my twenty year career to show the inside world of a police officer through stories that are sometimes tragic, dark, inappropriate, but still funny. Dark Knights can be found on Amazon:

https://www.amazon.com/dp/B0711CB8K2

I have spent my entire adult life in law enforcement and security, retiring from the NYPD at the rank of Captain. I began writing about two years ago and published several non-fiction titles dealing mainly with my law enforcement career.

C-CASE: is the story of the two years I was drafted as a lieutenant into the NYPD Internal Affairs Bureau.

https://www.amazon.com/dp/B07G8JMKRP

WHY ME? is a research based work inspired by my interactions with crime victims. Many people do not realize that there are specific things that they may do or not do that can make them and their homes attractive targets for criminals.

https://www.amazon.com/dp/B01N19KF2E

CONDUCTOR: is a change of pace from my law enforcement themed books. In 2013 my son was hired as a conductor with the Long Island Railroad. I was amazed at the amount of training required to become a federally qualified conductor. The book traces the history of this fabled profession, and provides insights for aspiring conductors.

https://www.amazon.com/Conductor-Railroad-Robert-L-Bryan-ebook/dp/B01N5QNT6Q

THE LAST DAY is my first work of fiction. It tells the story of a terrorist plot against the New York City subway system. The Last Day won the first place award for published fiction in the 2018 Public Safety Writers Association writing competition.

https://www.amazon.com/dp/B07856QWT4

You can check out all my books on my Amazon Author Page and website. Again, thanks, and I hope you enjoy Dark Knights 2. I would greatly appreciate a brief review when you have completed the book.

https://www.amazon.com/Robert-L.-Bryan/e/B01LXUSALG/ref=dp_byline_cont_ebooks_1

http://www.authorsexpresspromotion.net/robert-l-bryan

Dedicated to Marilyn, Bryan, and Meghan, who will always be the angel on my shoulder

CONTENTS

PROLOGUE:	The American Dream	9
INTRODUCTION:	The Chase	17
CHAPTER 1:	The Mall	25
CHAPTER 2:	Green Devils	32
CHAPTER 3:	Chula	48
CHAPTER 4:	71 Badge & Gun	61
CHAPTER 5:	Mean Green	67
CHAPTER 6:	The Rodeo	76
CHAPTER 7:	Gods Among Us	79
CHAPTER 8:	La Llorona	97

CHAPTER 9:	Line Watch	102
CHAPTER 10:	Nightlife	110
CHAPTER 11:	Standing Room Only	117
CHAPTER 12:	The Sign	124
CHAPTER 13:	C&Es	137
CHAPTER 14:	North	156
CHAPTER 15:	Call of the Wild	166
CHAPTER 16:	Searchlight	184
CHAPTER 17:	Crazy	191
CHAPTER 18:	Train Patrol	197
CHAPTER 19:	More Rails	204
CHAPTER 20:	Nude Beach	210

CHAPTER 21:	Uninvited Guests	224
CHAPTER 22:	Tonk	233
CHAPTER 23:	Shortcuts	242
CHAPTER 24:	Deadly Pursuits	250
CHAPTER 25:	Paranoia	263
CHAPTER 26:	The Interview	287
CHAPTER 27:	Still in Pursuit	299
CHAPTER 28:	Salvation	308
CHAPTER 29:	Home	320
EPILOGUE:	The Ironic Twist	325

PROLOGUE: THE AMERICAN DREAM

It's been said that borders, language, and culture are the essential elements of nationhood.

Borders define the physical space a nation lives in the same way the property line around our homes or the walls of our apartments define the space that is ours. Within this space, we define and enforce the standards and conditions of our lives. We may still care about those who exist outside our space, and we may try to help others in need, but at the end of the day we go home. We don't tolerate uninvited guests.

Obviously, I believe in a secure border and I believe in the United States Border Patrol. The men and women of the Border Patrol perform the most thankless and dangerous law enforcement job in America. They deal with alien smugglers, drug smugglers, and terrorists in the most challenging physical environments. The job of a patrol agent, however, is also the ultimate anomaly. It is a saga of heroism and sacrifice wrapped around a Greek tragedy.

While training for encounters with dangerous criminals, the daily reality is that most of their enforcement actions are taken against a non-criminal element. I know what some of you are thinking at this point. What does he mean – non-criminal element? Isn't entering this country illegally against the law? Of course it's against the law to enter this country illegally. When I refer to a non-criminal element, I'm not referring to smugglers, bandits or terrorists. I'm talking about the average person looking for a better life for their family, whose only crime was being born into horrendous conditions of poverty – conditions that if you or I were born into would most likely prompt the same trip north, regardless of the illegality.

What possible relevance could a philosophical rant about the border and illegal immigration have from an author whose prior books focused mainly on the New York City Police Department and New York City Transit Police Department? Well, I'll tell you.

Immediately after I retired from the New York City Police Department in 2001, I began work on my first book. I titled the book C-CASE, and it was to be a non-fictional account of a two-year portion of my twenty-year career. I suppose I was like a distance runner who had not trained properly for a race. I broke out of the starting gate in great form, but after a while I lost steam, and eventually I stopped. C-CASE was shelved indefinitely. In 2016 I finally got back on track and finished the race. C-CASE was complete. I followed the traditional publishing route, which I found very frustrating. From the time I turned the finished manuscript over to my publisher, it took approximately nine months for C-CASE to be published. While I waited, to keep myself busy – I wrote. Over a six-month period, almost as an afterthought, I completed another book. This work of non-fiction spanned my entire twenty-year career. I titled this book DARK KNIGHTS because it was a compilation of stories throughout the various stages of my career – from police officer to captain – that illustrated the humorous side of police work, usually through a very dark brand of humor.

C-CASE was finally published in April, 2017 and a month later I self- published DARK KNIGHTS. Subsequently, I have self-published several other works of both non-fiction and fiction, but an interesting trend developed. While I have been satisfied with sales of all my books, DARK

KNIGHTS has been my most successful title. While I don't expect DARK KNIGHTS to make the New York Times best seller list anytime soon, it has remained flirting with the best seller list in its three Amazon categories since its publication. I have concluded that DARK KNIGHTS sells well and reviews well because it hits a nerve with both the police and non-police audience. Police work is serious business, and there are a plethora of books that describe this serious, dangerous, exciting, heroic, and sometimes tragic line of work. I chose a different path. Police work has been described as 95% routine, mundane work mixed in with 5% of excitement. I wrote about the 95% - the day to day existence of a police officer which although not usually exciting, was sometimes very funny, and almost always politically incorrect.

I discovered that I really loved to write, and I pumped out several other books including a non-fiction book on the history of the railroad conductor profession as well as THE LAST DAY, my work of fiction, which details a terrorist plot against the New York City subway system. The problem was that other than my name, there was no thread connecting my books. Every article I have read on successful writing urges the author to produce a series of books, rather than stand-alone works. That advice made complete sense to me so I began work on a sequel. About ten thousand words into the follow-up to THE LAST DAY, I was struck by a big bolt of common sense. DARK KNIGHTS sells much better than THE LAST DAY, so why am I laboring to produce a sequel to a book that doesn't sell as well. The logic was flawless. Instantly, production on the sequel to THE LAST DAY was shelved, and I began working on a sequel to DARK KNIGHTS.

Since I spanned my entire twenty year career, this sequel could not just be a continuation. I gave the subject matter much thought over several days until my path became clear. I had no story to offer after I retired from the NYPD, but perhaps there was a story to tell before my New York City police career. Fresh out of college in 1978, I accepted appointment as a United States Border Patrol Agent and spent two years working on the southern border. But was this a realistic topic for my prequel? It was challenging enough getting a full book out of a twenty-year career. The prospects of duplicating this challenge with only two years of material and a fading memory to work from did not seem very bright, but I had one huge advantage. Although limited in duration, my understanding of this very complicated and often misunderstood job did not come from books and research. I had actually lived it. Good fortune also came my way in the form of a faded blue folder I found tucked away in the bottom of an attic box containing Christmas decorations. The folder contained all my old Border Patrol records. I had not seen these documents in years, and I was amazed with how much documentation I had kept. I had my appointment notice, academy training schedule, academy grades, just about every report I wrote at my duty station, as well as photos and newspaper articles from my time at the academy and duty station. As I went through the photos and documents, the memories rushed into my brain like waves crashing into a beach. I began furiously writing notes to capture these mental images before my memories receded like the tide. When my rough outline was complete, I now had to answer the key question – did I have a book?

Not only did I believe that I had enough material for a book, but I discovered something fascinating. After outlining all the experiences I could remember in the Border Patrol, I realized I likely had experienced as much excitement in two years on the Mexican border as I had during my entire twenty year New York City police career. I also recalled a certain sadness that came along with the job.

I am no fan of amnesty or sanctuary cities. There is a legal process required to enter this country and that process should be followed. Those who do not follow that process and enter illegally should be apprehended and removed. The sadness emanates from the human element. A patrol agent would have no feelings to remain unaffected by the tragic human story playing out on the southern border. That tragedy was best summed up to me many years ago, and it is still relevant today. I had just graduated from the Border Patrol Academy, and during my first week at my duty station I had a conversation with a veteran agent. He was a tall, stocky good ol' boy from Alabama who was 35-years of age, with a thick mane of premature snow white hair. He had been with the Border Patrol for nine years and was a stereotypical man's man, who had been a helicopter door gunner in Viet Nam. Accordingly, his world view meter was fixed on its most conservative setting. Despite this mindset, I still remember him attempting to explain the job to a young kid from New York City in his pronounced southern drawl.

"It's very hard to make this job look pretty, son. We live in the greatest country on earth, and most of the people we run into are just trying to grab a little piece of our American Dream. Unfortunately, it's our job to stop that dream. That's what we do every day."

With the realization that my two-year Border Patrol career was a pretty wild time -DARK KNIGHTS 2 – BORDER PATROL EDITION was born. All the stories are true. With the exception of some figures with historical significance, however, all the names have been changed. I hope you enjoy.

INTRODUCTION: THE CHASE

The farm resembled a magnificent rainforest from afar, with huge lush-green trees neatly growing in straight lines. There was no time to take in the beauty of the scene. The only senses my brain could currently deal with were my rapid, gasping breaths along with the hollow clomping sounds each time one of my heavy boots dug into a section of dirt road. Perhaps it was the lack of oxygen to the brain - the result of attempting to maintain a sprinter's pace for over ten minutes – that was creating a surreal landscape. I could no longer see or feel the blazing Southern California sun. Even though the dirt road had not narrowed, I had a feeling that the trees surrounding me on both sides were closing in, creating a seemingly endless tunnel through their lush, rainforest-like canopy effect. My body was urging me to quit, but my mind would not allow the embarrassment. I pushed forward straining to maintain a maximum sprint that had in reality transformed into nothing more than a slow trot. Was I gaining ground? I wasn't sure.

It didn't help matters that I was holding a Stetson cowboy hat in my right hand, slowing me down as it swung back and forth with each stride and creating wind resistance to my progress. Why didn't I leave that stupid hat in the vehicle? I was also becoming conscious of all the dirt I was kicking up as I labored down the dry road. I had become like the Pig-Pen character in the Peanuts comic strip, with a little tornado of dirt engulfing me as I ran. The dirt had already created a film on my dark green rough duty uniform and I was starting to cough as I inhaled the particles.

I was not going to be able to keep up the chase for much longer. Six months earlier I was sitting in a New York City bar, rejoicing with the rest of the inebriated patrons when Thurman Munson squeezed Ron Cey's foul pop-up securely into his catcher's mitt, giving the Yankees their second straight World Series championship, both victories coming over the Los Angeles Dodgers. Now, here I was, not too far from Dodger country, dressed up like some half-assed cowboy as I was about to pass out from exhaustion in the middle of an avocado farm. How the hell did I end up here?

Rewind approximately fifteen minutes. Agent Rich Coffey was driving the light green Border Patrol Dodge

Ram Charger. Coffey was a tall, barrel-chested, burly White male with a handle bar moustache who hailed from Tucson, Arizona. He was 52-years old, but surprisingly, he had only been with the border patrol for seven years. Agent Coffey had retired after a twenty year career in the Air Force at the rank of lieutenant colonel. He had been a combat pilot in Viet Nam and was now working on his second pension from Uncle Sam.

We had entered the avocado farm from the east. Other units were entering from the north, south and west. Coffey drove slowly down the access road and up to a barn. When we cleared the barn an avocado grove became visible. At the corner of the grove, a crew was hard at work picking avocados. The group hadn't noticed us as they toiled in the early afternoon sun. Equipped with a 20-foot tall pole that had a rucksack on the end, one of the men ascended into the treetops. Using one hand for stability on the teetering ladder, he swung his body out. In one fluid motion he snapped an avocado bunch and put it into the giant canvas bag that was slung over his small frame. The ritual was broken by the shriek of someone in the work crew, "LA MIGRA"

It took just a few scant seconds for airborne workers to be out of the treetops, and the entire crew of eight was frantically sprinting west on the dirt road that bisected the rows of avocado trees.

The Ram Charger could have easily navigated the ten foot wide dirt road, but Agent Coffey left the transmission in park. Instead, he turned in his seat and stared directly at me with a look as serious as cancer, as he stated in an annoyed and sarcastic tone. "Well, we're waiting"

Approximately two years later these same words would cause me to almost fall out of my seat in a New York City movie theatre. With the Border Patrol still a very fresh memory, I went to the movies to see the comedy, Caddyshack. There is a scene near the end of the movie where the Ted Knight character is impatiently waiting for a golfer to putt, until he finally says "Well, we're waiting." Anyone who knows what I am talking about knows exactly how Agent Coffey sounded to me.

No other words were necessary. I was out of the vehicle and running down the dirt road. There was an intersection in the road ahead. Some of the fleeing group turned right, others turned left, and two men remained running straight ahead on the path.

It has long been held that predators preferentially take the young, elderly, weak and diseased prey. This concept is central to natural selection and is one of the tenets on which evolution rests. In other words, predators don't play fair, and in the predatory role that had been thrust upon me, fairness was the last thing on my mind. The group was about 25-yards ahead when they broke into different directions. I maintained focus on the two males still in sight – the ones who had continued running straight on the road. In an instant I was sizing up my prey. One male appeared to be young and lean, while the other appeared older – maybe in his early forties, with a protruding pot belly that was visible even from my current distance. Another intersection was approaching. The young male made a left turn while my pot-bellied prey turned right. Natural selection made my decision easy. I turned right and continued stalking the weaker prey.

Back to the moment of rewind with my lungs about to burst. It was depressing that a 22-year old who believed he was in excellent physical condition, was considering giving up the pursuit of this short, overweight, 40-something illegal alien. I was just about ready to give up the chase and face the scorn of Agent Coffey, when my weakened prey made a move of desperation. The male must have reached his physical limit, as he darted off the dirt road and into the grove of avocado trees. I stopped at the point where my prey had left the road and stood for a few moments slumped over forward, with my hands on my knees, desperately trying to catch my breath. When I could finally straighten up and take a few normal breaths, I scanned the thick rows of trees and listened. Nothing. I tread cautiously into the thick grove of trees.

The white t-shirt stood out against the dark atmosphere created by the tree foliage and soil. He was face down and perfectly still, probably praying that La Migra would pass him by. My tap on the shoulder shattered his dreams. The portly male rolled on his side and looked sheepishly up at me. "Lo siento, senor."

I waved my right hand to indicate that no apology was necessary. "Esta bien, amigo." I then extended my right hand, which my prey gladly accepted as assistance to his feet.

"Gracias, senor."

"Come se llama, amigo"

"Diego, senor"

I placed my right hand on Diego's left shoulder to guide him out from the trees.

"Vamanos, Diego!"

When we were on the dirt road, I motioned that we were going to walk east. I spoke to Diego during what had now transitioned into a leisurely stroll. He was 42-years old and from Oaxaca. Oaxaqueños are folks from one of the Southern most states of Mexico. A large portion of these folks are fully Native American. Those like Diego, who hailed from the Capital, usually came from lineage that was more racially mixed with Spaniards. Diego stated that he had a wife and three children back in Oaxaca. He said that he came to America because there was no work to support his family in Mexico. Diego lamented that he had not seen his family in over two years, but that he sends just about all the money he earns to his wife each month. In just over two years he estimated that he had been caught by La Migra eight to twelve times. He said that each time a bus just dropped him off at the port of entry and he was ushered through iron gates into Tijuana. Diego slightly chuckled when he said that he was usually back in America within 24-hours.

The distant sound of a vehicle engine joined our conversation. The drone increased in volume until the light green Ram Charger turned onto the path in front of us. Agent Coffey did not say a word as he opened the tailgate of the vehicle. After a quick frisk he motioned for Diego to climb inside. With the prisoner secure, I was finally able to rest in the passenger seat in my dirt covered, sweat soaked uniform, Agent Coffey carefully made a U-turn and headed for the exit of the farm. He slapped my left knee and nodded his head in approval, "Good job, son!"

I stared straight ahead. I guess I should be proud. Because of me, a little piece of America was safe that day.

THE MALL

Winter, 1976: Queens Center Mall, New York City

I worked my way through the rack of flannel shirts, every so often removing a hangar to make a closer inspection of a product. I held the red plaid shirt at arms-length, evaluating how it may look on me. In reality, my attention was directed approximately fifty feet beyond the shirt.

A distinguished looking gentleman browsed at the display of men's leather jackets. The middle age male with short salt & pepper hair was meticulously groomed, complete with tweed sport coat, white shirt and brown print tie. He was probably a lawyer or an accountant doing some shopping on his lunch break. But there was something about his eyes. Every few seconds his eyes would lose focus on the jackets and dart back and forth, searching the surrounding area for something. I had seen these eyes many times before. It was my job to recognize these eyes. Any store detective worth his salt knew that those darting eyes were a primary sign that a theft was about to occur. It was just human nature for a thief to scan the area all around him before doing the deed.

I had worked as a store detective in Abraham & Strauss department store for about year and a half. For a college student with law enforcement aspirations, it was a great job while obtaining a degree in criminal justice. Instead of ringing up a cash register or stacking pallets of stock, I was roaming the store in the guise of a shopper, seeking out my prey – the shoplifter.

On this chilly early afternoon in the Queens Center Mall, I had the feeling I was about to hook a big one. This suave looking fellow was not your run-of-the-mill snatch and run thief. He may be a pro, and likely to hit big. If he was a professional, however, he would be very wary of surveillance, so I had to be careful not to spook him. I casually strolled into the corner of the men's department and when I was sure that the darting eyes were not darting towards me I ducked into the department's stock room. Two steps at a time I clanged up the metal staircase to the stock room mezzanine. At the top of the stairs I stopped. Adjacent to where I was standing there was a loose piece of ceiling tile at the point where the wall met the ceiling.

This loose tile was not a defect. In this era well before CCTV, a slight re-positioning of the tile allowed me to surreptitiously view the men's department selling floor. My subject was still pacing around the leather jackets and I was feeling more and more that he was about to bite at my hook.

I was carrying a small A&S bag that contained a walkie-talkie radio. The security department had one other radio, but I did not know who was carrying it at that time.

"Unit 1 to Unit 2 come in." My radio crackled.

"Go ahead unit 1."

"I'm in the men's department coop. I have eyes on a male/white 40 to 45, brown sport coat and tie. He looks like he's getting ready to hit for a leather jacket."

More crackle. "OK Cheech, I'll be by the Queens Blvd. doors."

Oh no! Cheech was the signature catchphrase of Juan Morales, a store detective who had been hired only two months earlier, and who had managed to become universally despised by all the other detectives in that short period of time. From the moment he arrived he was constantly pushing and prodding where he didn't belong. A few months earlier, one of the security guards who worked overnight had been caught filling his car on the loading dock with all types of merchandise. Juan was constantly asking me, and anyone else he could corner, about the theft. He would throw out how easy it would be to steal from the store. I guess he wanted to see what kind of a reaction he would get. I gave him no reaction and did the best I could to avoid any conversation with him.

The consensus of the security department was that Juan was either a thief or an undercover agent sent in to try to find a thief. Either way, I didn't like him.

Because leather jackets were expensive, a strong wire was run through the sleeves of all the jackets on a rack. If a customer wanted to try a jacket on, he would have to get a salesperson to open the lock and remove the jacket from the wire.

My wait in the coop didn't last long. My subject displayed his darting eyes one more time before producing wire cutters from his pocket. In one fluid movement he cut the wire and removed not one, not two, but three leather jackets from the rack. In less than ten seconds the jackets were off the rack, folded, and stuffed into the large shopping bag he was carrying. The subject worked his way through the racks of clothing and made a right turn on the main aisle.

I was on the radio. "He's coming towards you now. He hit for three jackets. They're in his shopping bag."

More crackle. "I'm on it Cheech."

I was down the metal steps, out of the stockroom and out to the main aisle. I ran toward the Queens Blvd. exit doors in time to see Juan walking with my subject in tow. When we got back to the security office Juan very generously volunteered to begin filling out the apprehension paperwork while I returned to the men's department. I wanted to retrieve the tags he had ripped off the jackets and to tell the department manager to take the rack of jackets out of service until the cut wire could be replaced.

I returned to the security office to find Juan typing furiously at a desk, with the subject sitting head down on an adjacent wood bench, his right hand handcuffed to an I-bolt in the bench.

I stood behind Juan, "OK, I'll take it from here."

He stopped typing but did not vacate the chair. I could see over his shoulder that he had just about completed the first apprehension form. Next to the caption "Apprehending Detective" was typed in all caps JUAN MORALES. Son of a bitch. Not only was this guy probably stealing from the store, now, he was going to try to steal my case.

I am sure that by now you are checking to see if you bought the correct book. What does my journey to the Mexican border have to do with a department store in Queens, New York City? All I can say right now is hang in there.

An ironic twist is a literary technique that introduces a radical change in the direction or expected outcome of the plot. It may change the audience's perception of the preceding events, or introduce a new conflict that places it in a different context. A plot twist may be foreshadowed to prepare the audience to accept it. Now that I've completed my best foreshadowing – on with the story. If you want to find out about the bizarre plot twist, you're just going to have to keep reading.

GREEN DEVILS

Growing up, I never had any great desire to become a cop. Law enforcement was not a family tradition and except for one cousin, I had no police officers in the family. Furthermore, my formative years during the 1960s and 1970s were spent in the very middle-class neighborhood of Jackson Heights, Queens, where there was rarely, if ever, any need for police intervention, and there was no friendly Officer Joe walking a beat nearby. My entire knowledge and perception of law enforcement came from watching TV shows like Adam 12 and Dragnet.

As I prepared to enter college I had never even heard of the United States Border Patrol. With no clear career path I enrolled at St. John's University, majoring in criminal justice for no reason other than it seemed to be a very easy major. After all, I wanted a college degree, but I really didn't want to work hard to achieve it. Speaking of work, my parents were finally insisting that I find a job while I attended college. My sister, who is two years older than me, was working at the newly opened Queens Center

Mall, and she was dating a guy who was working in the security department of Abraham & Strauss department store. My parents proceeded to lean heavily on my sister's boyfriend to get a job for me at the store. This is how I landed as a store detective.

There were about twenty other store detectives in the security department and at least fifteen of them were also college students, but I was the only one attending St. John's. The remainder of my coworkers were students at John Jay College of Criminal Justice, the gold standard for criminal justice education. My social world began to revolve around my friends from the store, all whom had aspirations of becoming police officers.

While hanging out after work, aside from the normal 18-22 year old drinking and carousing, conversations would inevitably lead to topics involving law enforcement jobs. Whether I liked it or not I was current on every law enforcement civil service test coming up just from being involved in the conversations. I simply became caught up in their enthusiasm.

Contributing greatly to my newfound purpose in life was my father. My dad had no great interest in seeing his son become a cop, but he was a huge cheerleader for the civil service system. A high school dropout who went to sea as a merchant marine at sixteen years of age, my dad returned to dry land only to be drafted into
the Army for the Korean War. At the conclusion of the conflict, he found himself back home in New York City without a job or a high school diploma. He was able to pass a civil service test for stationery fireman, which he qualified for because of his experience tending to the boilers on ships, and he was eventually hired by the NYC Sanitation Department. A number of years later, he passed a promotional
exam and was appointed a stationery engineer. To anyone who would listen, my dad would happily espouse the universal truth that only through the civil service system could a high school dropout like him end up with a good job and great benefits. Even though I was not a high school dropout and would soon possess a college degree, he pushed me to take every civil service exam that I qualified

for, both law enforcement and non–law enforcement. The Chief-Leader was the local civil service newspaper, and it was required reading at my house.

The Chief was a weekly newspaper that came out every Tuesday. I distinctly remember visiting the stationary store in the local shopping center on a Tuesday during my senior year in college, and picking up the latest edition of the Chief. As I waited in line to pay for the paper, I read the bold headline on page one: US BORDER PATROL AGENT TEST IN NYC. I went outside to my car and immediately began reading the details. Since I knew absolutely nothing about the Border Patrol, I was very interested in the story's description of what a Border Patrol Agent did. I still have that fateful issue of the Chief newspaper among my Border Patrol documents, and the article read in part:

The primary functions of the United States Border Patrol are the enforcement of the immigration and nationality laws and the corresponding criminal code and the apprehension of violators of these and related laws within the jurisdiction of the Immigration and Naturalization Service. To accomplish these functions Border Patrol Agents perform on a rotational basis a number of basic duties which may vary from one part of the country to another because of local operating requirements, geographical considerations, including isolation, and program goals and objectives. Duties typical of the Border Patrol occupation are International Boundary Security Control Operations, Sign Cutting, Farm and Ranch Check, Traffic and Transportation Check, City Patrol, Boat Patrol, Crewman Control, and Anti-Smuggling Operations.

As a soon to be college graduate, I could figure out what most of these duties involved, but one duty in particular was perplexing me – sign cutting. I had visions of agents standing near the border at work benches with safety glasses and saws, laboring to cut through signs. Why would they be doing that? Oh well, I was just going to take this test as a lark, so I would probably never have to find out what kinds of signs needed to be sawed in half.

I filed to take the test and approximately a month later I sat in a large testing room in a federal building on Varick Street in Manhattan and completed the Border Patrol Agent written test. They say everyone has a talent, and one of mine happened to be that I was a good test taker. This skill served me well during my rise to the rank of police captain in my post Border Patrol career, but my first success in testing was on the Border Patrol exam, on which I scored 95 percent.

About a month and a half after receiving the exam results, I received a notice to appear for an oral examination, also at the federal building on Varick Street. I had received approximately two weeks lead time to appear for the oral test, and all during that time period my dad had incessantly cautioned me not to appear at any interview setting with the full beard I had so proudly developed over the prior few months. I completely ignored his warnings right up until the moment I stepped out of the shower on the morning of the exam. I gazed into the mirror and for the first time considered that he may be right. With time becoming a factor I trimmed my beard with a scissors as close as possible, and then the real fun began. Before I began working with the scissors I had neglected to confirm the presence of an operable razor. There was none – only my dad's electric razor. Do you know what it's like to try to shave a beard with an electric razor? Besides being extremely painful, it can't be done – but I sure tried. I reached the point where I had thick blotches of whiskers over several parts of my face and chin, and the parts that were whisker free were red and bleeding. I finally decided that I could waste no more time. I stopped the bleeding, put on my suit and left for Manhattan.

The two interviewers conducting the exam were very large, intimidating looking middle age males, who identified themselves as Supervisory Border Patrol Agents from somewhere in Texas. They had the look of grizzled Border Patrol veterans, despite the fact that they both wore business suits. Once I was seated alone in the room with the examiners, there was a moment of very uncomfortable silence while they attempted to assess who or what it was they had seated before them. Finally, one of the agents broke the silence in a very deliberate drawl, "What the hell happened to your face, son?"

I sighed deeply and told the sordid tale of the scissors and electric razor. The agents responded with blank stares and then began asking the examination questions. I don't remember any specific questions on the exam, other than that they were the problem solving situational type. I think the questions involved hypothetical emergency situations where I had to find a solution to finding an alien in the desert, dealing with a man with a gun, and handling an accident involving a truckload full of illegal aliens. I remember leaving the building feeling that I had answered the exam questions appropriately, but that these good ol' Texas boys probably wanted nothing to do with this New York City boob who couldn't figure out how to shave properly.

The oral exam was pass/fail and I have to admit that I was mildly surprised when a few weeks later I received a letter from the Department of Justice with "Passed" stamped as the exam result.

At this point you might be asking why would a NYC boy who had not ventured much farther than Upstate New York be interested in moving to the Mexican border. Good question. The answer was twofold. As I approached college graduation in 1978, the prospects for a law enforcement career in the New York City area could not have been bleaker. US economic stagnation in the 1970s hit New York City particularly hard, amplified by a large movement of middle-class residents to the suburbs, which drained the city of tax revenue. New York City was on the brink of bankruptcy. On July 1, 1975, the City of New York laid off an initial 15,000 workers, including 3,000 cops and 1,600 firefighters – 20% of the city's entire force. Some 26 fire companies were simply disbanded. By September, 45,000 workers had been laid off. From July 1975 until November 1979, no police officers were hired or trained in the City of New York. The only "new" officers were those who had been laid off on July 1, 1975, and were rehired over the next three years.

The second reason for even considering a job with the Border Patrol was much more personal. All law enforcement jobs have physical and medical standards that must be met for appointment. I have worn glasses since I was twelve years old, so I was always very aware of the vision requirements for a job. Whenever I would read the requirements for a specific job I would always scan directly to the vision requirements.

The NYPD vision requirement at the time was 20/40 uncorrected. My vision wasn't horrible, but it was very questionable whether I would be able to read an eye chart at 20/40. The Border Patrol, on the other hand, had a 20/70 uncorrected vision requirement, and I knew I would be able to comply with that vision standard. So there you have it. A lack of opportunity combined with questionable vision made the Border Patrol an option. But after I graduated college and lounged my way through the summer of 1978, the Border Patrol had already moved out of the realm of conscious thought. Then one day near the end of September another letter arrived from the United States Department of Justice. It was a notice of appointment as a Border Patrol Agent with assignment to the Chula Vista, California sector. The EOD (entry on duty) date was one month in the future, and there was phone number to call to accept the appointment. I slightly chuckled before crumpling up the letter and tossing it in the kitchen trash. I then continued with my schedule for the day which currently involved watching television. Bill Haley's *Rock Around the Clock* signaled that another episode of Happy Days was about to begin, but my thoughts had drifted elsewhere. It suddenly hit me that the stars were lined up in a way that they probably never would be again. I was single, living at home, freshly out of college, and attached to absolutely nothing. I rose from the living room sofa and proceeded directly to the kitchen trash basket. I unraveled the crumpled paper and made the phone call.

Today's border patrol is very different than the agency I joined in 1978. Homeland Security became a primary concern of the nation after the terrorist attacks of September 11, 2001. On March 1st, 2003, the Border Patrol, formerly part of the Justice Department's

Immigration and Naturalization Service, along with four other Federal entities merged into Customs and Border Protection, under the Department of Homeland Security. In November 2005, the U.S. Border Patrol published an updated national strategy, including a more expanded role than solely apprehending illegal aliens. This updated strategy charged the Border Patrol with responsibilities beyond illegal immigration, including fighting terrorism, drug smuggling, and reducing crime in border communities. With 19,437 agents, the Border Patrol is one of the largest law enforcement agencies in the United States. In 1978, however, trying to find information about this agency I had just committed to join was not that easy.

As I scanned the card catalogue on a Saturday morning in October 1978 it was quickly becoming apparent that I would not be adding to my zero Border Patrol knowledge. There were no books in the entire library about the Border Patrol. Before departing defeated, I visited the librarian and whispered my dilemma to her. The pleasant looking middle age women never said a word before disappearing into a back office. I was beginning to consider that she may be ignoring me when she appeared back at her desk carrying a very large book. She appeared annoyed at causing such a loud "thump" when she dropped the book on her desk. "I think you may find some material on what you're looking for in this book."

It was not a book about the Border Patrol, but was titled *The History of Mexico*. I thanked the librarian before hauling the huge book to a nearby table, careful not to annoy her with another loud thud. I paid little to no attention to Mexico's history while paging through the huge book. My paging gained in speed, but suddenly came to an abrupt stop. I had come to a chapter on illegal immigration and I was now staring at numerous photos of Border Patrol Agents at work. There was also a somewhat detailed history of the Border Patrol.

The chapter detailed how seventy-five immigration inspectors on horseback first began enforcing immigration laws on the U.S.-Mexico border in 1904. The U.S.-Mexico border was not even formalized until the 1848 Treaty of Guadalupe Hidalgo ended the Mexican-American War.

Congress first established an independent Border Patrol as part of the restrictive Immigration Act of 1924; 450 employees were deployed along both U.S. land borders in response to illegal entries and alien smuggling. By 1930, the Border Patrol's size had nearly doubled, and additional growth ensued during World War II based on national security concerns.

When Prohibition went into effect, resources were diverted to stem the illicit flow of alcohol (particularly along the Canadian border). The 1933 repeal of Prohibition coincided with the Great Depression and reduced flows of undocumented labor into the United States, decreasing the demand for border enforcement during the 1930s.

With a few exceptions, border enforcement failed to rise again to national prominence in policy debates until the late 1970s. In part, this inattention reflected the fact that the majority of Mexico-U.S. migration from 1942 to 1964 was legal under the Bracero Program, which brought millions of Mexican workers to the United States to offset labor shortages, most of whom returned home seasonally.

Furthermore, Mexicans were able to enter the United States without quantitative limit prior to the 1965 amendments to the Immigration and Nationality Act. And it was not until 1976 that Congress extended the strict, 20,000 per-country limit and preference system to countries in the Western Hemisphere, including Mexico.

There were photos of agents on horseback and working at highway checkpoints. Some agents wore uniforms with cowboy type hats, while the agents at the highway checkpoints seemed to sport a more dress uniform attire, including campaign hats. I was fascinated by one particular photo. The black and white half page picture depicted a group of Mexican illegal aliens running along a riverbank. About twenty yards behind the group were three uniformed Border Patrol Agents in hot pursuit. The caption under the photo read simply *Group fleeing from green devils*. That caption stayed with me for a long time. How was I supposed to feel about being part of an agency known as green devils?

My decision to join the Border Patrol was met with the exact same response from all my friends and family –

derisive laughter. In retrospect, I could understand their disbelief. Up until that time, it was a big deal for me to take the subway into Manhattan, and now I had announced that I was headed to the southern border. Of course no one believed I was serious, and they continued to discount my intentions – right up to the moment my flight to San Diego took off from LaGuardia Airport. California, here I come.

CHULA

Unless I planned to camp out on the street outside the Chula Vista Border Patrol station, I needed to stay someplace for the night. In 1978 you could not just go online and quickly compare every hotel in a city, so I tried a much less technical option. I dialed long distance information for Chula Vista, California and asked to be connected with any hotel. I was connected with Motel 6 and made a reservation to spend my first night.

I arrived in San Diego in the early afternoon and took a cab from the airport to the motel in Chula Vista. Once I was settled in my room, I walked across the street to a burger joint and returned to my room with enough food to last the night.

The next morning I awoke bright and early to begin my new career. I believe the report time was 8:00 AM and because I was taking absolutely no chances of encountering any problems, I called for a cab to take me to the Border Patrol station at 6:30 AM. Without even being sworn in I had my first opportunity to feel foolish. I had simply called for the cab at the motel, and they never asked for my destination. I also never scouted out the location. All I had to give the cab driver was the address of the station. When I slid into the back seat of the cab, the elderly driver gave me a very odd look in the rear view mirror as I read the address off my appointment letter. Two blocks later the cab came to a stop. I was momentarily confused until I realized that we had reached the destination. If I had taken the time to scout the area or even ask someone at the motel, I would have discovered that the Border Patrol station was all of two blocks from the motel, a walk of less than five minutes.

Seeing that it was now only 6:35 AM, I was the first new agent to report. I was directed to an exterior location outside of what looked like a classroom or reception office and told to wait in an area containing several picnic tables. Little by little, more new agents started drifting to the picnic tables. When a Supervisory Border Patrol Agent ushered us into the reception office, there were a total of twenty new Border Patrol Agents to be sworn in.

My new classmates were from all over the country. California, Washington, Indiana, Illinois, Oregon, Oklahoma, and New York were among the states represented by the newly hired agents. For some reason, whenever I thought of the Border Patrol I always thought of Texas, and I found it odd that there were no Texans among my new classmates. What I did not realize was that while we went through our initial processing at Chula Vista, there was a group of newly hired agents being processed in the El Paso sector headquarters. They were just about all Texans and would meet us at the Federal Law Enforcement Training Center in Georgia in several days to become the 128th session of the United States Border Patrol Academy.

For the next two days we were processed through all the voluminous paperwork by an agent named Kevin Gorman. Kevin had been with the Border Patrol for about five years and was a Mormon from Utah. He was an extremely nice guy who contradicted my impression that the environment was going to be military-like with instructors screaming in my face. The environment for these first days in Chula Vista was very laid back and mellow. Boy, did that change when we got to Georgia.

All of my new classmates seemed sociable and friendly, but right from the beginning I would sometimes feel like I was an outsider in some club. This may have been some paranoia on my part, but I had several good reasons to feel that I didn't fit the mold of my Border Patrol class. First, I was the youngest in the group. I had just turned twenty two, with the closest age to me being twenty six. Most of the group were in their late twenties and early thirties. Next, only one other person in the group besides me had not served in the military. Additionally, I was one of two new agents who had not worked as a police officer and had qualified for the Border Patrol by virtue of a college degree. So, here I was, the youngest in a group of former cops and former military, with my only claim to fame being a college degree. Finally, I was from New York City. This was the first time I realized how some people from different parts of the country take an instant dislike to people from NYC. Don't get me wrong, no one was unsociable or hostile, but I just always had the sense of being an outsider among the former cops and military veterans. This is probably why I spent most of the processing days at Chula Vista hanging around with Steve Caridi.

Steve was twenty six years old, and was the other member of the class from New York City. Specifically, Steve was from the Bronx and he was the only other person in our group who qualified with a college degree, having no prior military or law enforcement experience. Steve was about 5'7" with a muscular build. Steve ended up being one of my roommates at the academy and I grew to like him a lot. I could also understand, however, how people could take an instant dislike to Steve. He typified that negative NYC stereotype – loud, abrasive, and opinionated. In retrospect, I believe I benefitted from Steve's personality. Even though I had spent my entire life to that point in New York City, my personality was the polar opposite of Steve's. I was reserved and shy, and preferred to melt into the crowd in a group situation. On numerous occasions during these initial days and at the academy I had classmates tell me that even though I was a New Yorker, I was a nice guy – not a jerk like Steve.

Steve's first episode occurred during the first day of processing. Kevin explained that we would be on probation for one year, and that our success in completing probation hinged on three factors. First, we would have to pass the 16- weeks of academy training at the Federal Law Enforcement Training Center in Georgia. He continued to say that once we started working at our duty stations, we would have to return to the Chula Vista sector headquarters at the 5.5 and 10 month points of employment to complete tests. Kevin said that these tests were known as the "five and a half and ten month tests" and that they were written exams in immigration law and Spanish. Kevin went on to say that the ten month test also included an oral Spanish exam conducted by a sector chief. He concluded the topic by stating that failure to pass the ten month test resulted in immediate termination from the Border Patrol.

Kevin stated that until we successfully completed the probation period, we were not Border Patrol Agents. After several seconds of blank stares from the assembled class, he clarified that we were Border Patrol Agent trainees. Kevin stated that from this point until the moment we completed probation, on every form where we had to list our name and title, we would write our title as BPA (t), with the small "t" in parenthesis emphasizing our low trainee status. Myself, and the rest of the class hated this procedure. It became especially galling after we graduated from the academy and still had to use (t) in our title at our duty stations while still on probation.

Steve wasted no time in voicing his displeasure. Kevin had just finished explaining the trainee designation when Steve's hand shot up in the air. He did not wait for Kevin to actually recognize him before blurting out very sarcastically, "Are you serious with this small t thing – this is ridiculous."

Kevin appeared somewhat stunned, but maintained his level, friendly demeanor while explaining to Steve that as ridiculous as it may seem to him, he would still have to comply.

Steve whispered to me, "I guess they want us to feel low and small, so I'll play along."

From that moment forward, on every form that required the trainee title to be listed after BPA, Steve inserted the smallest (t) that was humanly possible to write. On some of his forms, it appeared that a magnifying glass would be necessary to make out the (t). I can only imagine that no one really scrutinized the forms very closely, because during the next sixteen weeks, nobody ever said a word to Steve about his microscopic trainee t's.

During these first two days we also received our official duty station assignments. This was a complete surprise to me. I had been directed to report to the Chula Vista station, and I just assumed that I was to be assigned to Chula Vista. Most of the class was, in fact, assigned to the Chula Vista station. Two trainees, however, were assigned to the station at Temecula, California, and five trainees, including me, were assigned to the San Clemente station. San Clemente? San Clemente was nowhere near the border. What was I going to be doing there? It turned out that Temecula and San Clemente were traffic checkpoints.

The San Clemente checkpoint station was located sixty-six miles

north of the U.S.-Mexico border. It sat directly on the northbound lanes
of California's Interstate 5, the main highway that connects San Diego and Los Angeles. Agents of the U.S. Border Patrol conducted operations from a station adjacent to the highway. I didn't concern myself too much with the specifics of the assignment. I figured that in sixteen weeks I would know all about the Border Patrol operations at San Clemente.

At lunch time during day one at Chula Vista, Frank Monte, a former Marine and police officer from a suburb of Chicago, appointed himself class social director, and began arranging for everyone in the class to relocate to one nearby hotel so that we could double up in rooms and save on the cost. I went along with the program, and moved in for the next two days with Tom McCoy, a thirty-four year old former deputy sheriff from Washington State. Steve, of course, declined to participate in the roommate program and chose to remain alone in his original motel.

We were scheduled for three full days of processing at Chula Vista with a flight out of San Diego to the Federal

Law Enforcement Training Center on the morning of the fourth day. During the afternoon of the second day, we were driven to a store, which I think was in San Diego, to purchase uniforms. The Border Patrol uniform is a dark shade of green, but there are actually two distinct uniforms – rough duty and dress. The rough duty uniform consisted of a Stetson cowboy style hat to compliment green rough duty pants and shirt. The dress uniform had trousers with blue stripes and a campaign style hat. I was told that at San Clemente, the dress uniform was worn while working the highway checkpoint. At the end of the second day, Kevin Gorman informed us that he had an unanticipated problem. He stated that things had gone so smoothly that processing was complete even though we still had one more scheduled day. Kevin told us not to worry, and that he would surely find something for us to do in the morning.

The next morning found the entire class sweating in the hot sun right on the border line, about a quarter mile east of the San Ysidro port of entry. A flatbed truck had just pulled up next to us and two laborers began unloading fencing material off the back of the truck. It had been decided that the best way to keep us busy on this final day was to ship us down to the line and have us help erect a section of new fence. No one was particularly happy about this assignment, but Steve was beside himself. To anyone who would listen, Steve provided the same mantra. "This is bullshit. Trainee status or not, fence building is not in my job description."

Some classmates were sympathetic, while others just ignored him. A couple told Steve to shut up and get to work on the fence.

The two laborers on the truck had a very distinctive look. To be kind, I will say that they could have been descendants of the Hatfield's or McCoy's. Of Course Steve was going to have to voice his opinion. In 1972, the movie Deliverance, starring Burt Reynolds, was a huge box office hit. The film included a scene with some very perverted hillbilly types performing some very perverted acts. When the two laborers came out of the truck, Steve greeted them with a very loud, "Hey look over there. Right off the set of Deliverance."

The two laborers stared in Steve's direction, not knowing whether to smile or not through their gapped teeth.

As the morning dragged on, I found myself with Steve trying to determine whether one particular hole was deep enough to insert the fence post. Then, it happened. I heard a dull thudding sound followed immediately by Steve's screaming voice. "You motherfuckers!"

Steve was holding his left shoulder with his right hand, a large rock lying at his feet. Standing about twenty yards south of us were three Mexican males, who appeared to be anywhere from 14-18 years of age. They were laughing and hooting loudly, apparently very proud that one of their rocks had found its mark on Steve's shoulder. Steve took a couple of quick steps in the direction of the youths, but he was grabbed abruptly by his right arm. Al Norris had been a deputy with the San Diego County Sheriff's Department, and his message to Steve was crystal clear. "Hey asshole, you're walking into another country. You want to cause an international incident?"

Steve was quick to respond while pulling out of Al's grasp. "I don't care what country it is. Somebody hits me with a rock and they catch a beating – simple as that."

Before Steve could continue his trek into Mexico, one of the Deliverance boys unexpectedly chimed in. "You go ahead boy. You run off into TJ after them kids," he stated using the slang for Tijuana. "They'll drag you off and you'll never be heard from again. So you go ahead boy."

Deliverance waved his hand to the south, as if to encourage Steve to cross into Mexico. Steve sighed and then picked up the rock that had been used on him. He hurled it over the border, but came nowhere near the retreating youths. Steve turned his attention back to the fence pole and mumbled to no one in particular, "I told you this was not in our job description."

The following morning we boarded a flight in San Diego for our non-stop trip to Jacksonville, Florida. It was already dark when our bus pulled into the Federal Law Enforcement Training Center.

71 BADGE & GUN

The Federal Law Enforcement Training Center (FLETC) serves as an interagency law enforcement training body for 91 federal law enforcement agencies. It also provides training to state, local, campus, tribal, and international law enforcement agencies.

The FLETC headquarters are at the former Naval Air Station in the Glynco area of unincorporated Glynn County, Georgia, near the port city of Brunswick, Georgia, and about halfway between Savannah, Georgia and Jacksonville, Florida.

Studies conducted in the late 1960s revealed an urgent need for training by professional instructors using modern training facilities and standardized course content. The permanent location of the center was originally planned for the Washington, D.C. area. However, a three-year construction delay resulted in Congress requesting that surplus federal installations be surveyed to determine if one could serve as the permanent site. In May 1975, after a review of existing facilities, the Glynco site was selected.

In the summer of 1975, the new Federal Law Enforcement Training Center relocated from Washington, D.C., and began training in September of that year at Glynco. The facility was just over three years old when twenty Border Patrol trainees arrived from Chula Vista and were joined by twelve trainees from El Paso to form the 128th session of the United States Border Patrol Academy.

To a kid from New York City, the center appeared to be mostly a heavily wooded forest. Spread out among the 1,600 acres were the facilities, including buildings for administration, classrooms and training, dining, dormitories, instructor offices, gymnasium, student center, convenience store, auditorium, outdoor firing range, driver training range, swimming pool and athletic field.

It took all of about five minutes for me to become confused after arriving at FLETC. It seemed that besides being the 128th session of the Border Patrol Academy, my class was also the 185th session of the Police Training Division. What? It seemed that two types of training were being combined in my academy class. The Treasury Department ran FLETC and Treasury Department instructional staff comprised the Police Training Division. The Border Patrol, however, detailed their own personnel to FLETC to serve as instructors for the Border Patrol specific training topics, specifically, Spanish, immigration law, firearms, and physical training. The more generic law enforcement topics were handled by the FLETC instructors. Upon graduation, I actually received two diplomas – one for completion of the Border Patrol Academy and the other for completion of the Center conducted portion of the basic course of instruction in law enforcement and police techniques

That first night at FLETC the only activity involved issuing the class their housing assignments. We were housed in very nice two-story townhomes that were located about a half mile from the instructional complex. The second floor of the townhomes had three bedrooms with the first floor consisting of a kitchen and living room. The first floor, however, was completely closed off, giving trainees access only to the second floor bedrooms. With three bedrooms, there were three trainees assigned to a townhome. By luck (or curse) of the draw, Steve was one of my roommates. My other roommate was Alan Wilson, a 27-year old from San Francisco who had been a military policeman in the Army for four years.

The next morning the actual 16-week training schedule commenced, beginning with health screening, orientation, distribution of study materials, and the Spanish placement test. Also commencing was the more structured, disciplined environment. Don't get me wrong – no one was ever running around screaming in my face making me do punishment push-ups, but there was a very militaristic atmosphere to our entire academy structure.

On the first day of class, the 128th sat for the first time together as a group. Supervisory Agent Don Anderson, the lead instructor for our class explained what was expected from us over the next sixteen weeks. As he went over the curriculum, I noticed that something had been boldly written in chalk on the board behind him - *71 Badge & Gun.* What the heck did that mean? Was that some Border Patrol motto? Could it be the Border Patrol's version of the Marines Semper Fi do or die?

On this opening day, we were also given a Spanish placement test and broken into three groups for Spanish classes. The first group consisted of native Spanish speakers. Honestly, I don't really know what the native speakers did in Spanish class for the next 16-weeks. Obviously, the native speakers must have found the academy far less intense than the rest of us. The second group, to which I was assigned, were the intermediate Spanish speakers. Intermediate meant that we had a couple of years of high school Spanish and could identify "como se llama" as what is your name? The final group were known as the sweat hogs. These were the trainees who were starting off their language training not knowing what adios and si meant.

By the end of the day we were broken up into our Spanish groups. My group happened to be in the room where the first briefing from Supervisory Agent Anderson had taken place. Agent Victor Delgado, our Spanish instructor, was getting ready to dismiss us for the day. I knew I was not the only trainee anticipating dinner, but we had to delay our exit until Agent Delgado gave the word. "Any questions?"

Everyone was already leaning out of their chairs, anticipating that the next word would be *Dismissed*. A couple of trainees almost fell over anticipating a dismissal that didn't come. Instead, Agent Delgado responded to a hand that had shot up from the back of the classroom. Dave Benson was a 28-year old former deputy sheriff from Greenville, Mississippi. Dave spoke apologetically, "I'm sorry to be holding everyone up from running to the mess hall but I just have to know what that means."

Agent Delgado had a confused look on his face but Dave clarified the question when he pointed to the *71 Badge & Gun* still boldly displayed on the blackboard. "Oh, that," Delgado chuckled. "That means if you attain at least a 71 average on all your academy classes you graduate and get your badge and gun. DISMISSED!"

As I made my way with the group toward the mess hall I reflected on this Border Patrol saying or motto. It really encouraged a trainee to shoot for the stars, didn't it? What a credo. Just barely pass and that's good enough for government work. I could never figure out why the motto used 71 when 70 was the minimum passing score. I guess it was because 71 rhymed with gun. Oh well, it was time for dinner.

MEAN GREEN

There was a lot of training taking place at FLETC besides our class. The Border Patrol itself, had several other training operations ongoing. The 125th, 126th, and 127th sessions were in various stages of academy training when we arrived. Additionally, there were immigration inspectors, US park police officers, customs inspectors, federal protective officers, and criminal investigators going through training. What created a stark contrast from the Border Patrol and all the other training was the fact that the Border Patrol classes marched in formation everywhere. We marched to the various classrooms and training facilities, and we marched to and from the mess hall for our meals. During physical training we ran in formation. There was also much "cadence calling" while we marched and ran, which in looking back, provided subtle insight into the nature of the Border Patrol organization.

In the armed services, a military cadence, or cadence call is a traditional call-and-response work song sung by military personnel while running or marching. Many cadences have a call and response structure in which one soldier initiates a line, and the remaining soldiers complete it, thus instilling teamwork and camaraderie for completion. The cadence calls move to the beat and rhythm of the normal speed (quick time) march or running-in-formation (double time) march. This serves the purpose of keeping soldiers "dressed", moving in step as a unit and in formation, while maintaining the correct beat or cadence.

The first marching cadence calls we were taught, and probably our most common chant as we marched around the complex was sung in the traditional call-and-response structure. It went like this:

Everywhere we go

People want to know

Who we are

So we tell them

We are the MEAN GREEN

Mighty, mighty MEAN GREEN

Wet-catching green machine

I guess there are a couple of lines in that short chant that those in the politically correct world may take umbrage with. I knew from my library research that I was a green devil, but what was mean green? I soon learned that mean green was a nickname fully endorsed by the Border Patrol. The base convenience store was filled with mean green shirts, caps, and cups. But what exactly did it mean to be mean green? It certainly had a macho ring to it. Steve, as usual, had his own unique perspective on the topic. Steve was a paradox. On one hand, he was a very loud street guy from the Bronx, with an opinion on everything. On the other hand, Steve turned out to be one of the most well-read, knowledgeable, and cerebral people I had ever met. When we completed our first "mean green" chant, Steve looked at me and said, "Mean green? What the fuck is that supposed to mean? Are we supposed to be mean to the aliens? Are we mean-spirited? Do we have a mean streak? And I guess we can call them wetbacks since we're singing the term in the song, right?"

He didn't wait for my opinion, but instead let out a loud laugh, obviously pleased with his commentary.

Another chant that garnered the wrath of Steve was a running cadence. Again it used a call-and-response structure, and it used the term PA, which was short for patrol agent. PA, however, was not the term that got Steve all worked-up. The cadence went like this:

PA, PA, where you been

I been to the river and back again

PA, PA, what did you see

I saw a senorita, looking at me

PA, PA, what did you do

No, no Jefe, not a tellin' you

Steve's commentary was brutally blunt. "So I guess we're allowed to have sex with the Mexican girls while we patrol by the river, right? That's what the song is inferring, right?"

Again, my opinion was not required as Steve broke out into his self-satisfied laughter.

Crammed in around all the marching, running and singing was 16-weeks of training. Having subsequently completed recruit police training in New York City and later serving as an instructor at the NYPD police academy at the police officer and sergeant ranks, I believe I can speak with a degree of authority in saying that the Border Patrol training was far more intense than any of my academy experiences in NYC. The number one factor contributing to the intensity level was the necessity to learn a new language in 16-weeks.

The most intense training for the non-Spanish speakers was the 200 hours of Spanish, followed closely by the 130 hours of Immigration, Nationality, Constitutional, and Criminal Law.

There was no Spanish and immigration law training in the New York City Police Academy, but what really set the training programs apart were the firearms and physical training. During my era, NYPD recruits were trained at the range for one week before they qualified. In the

Border Patrol Academy we had firearms training every other day for ten weeks before qualifying in a standard qualification course and a practical pistol course. We also had to show proficiency with a shotgun and during night fire, by using the muzzle flash to line up the sights for the next shot. Additionally we had to simulate a disabled shooting arm, and successfully load and fire our Smith & Wesson Model 66 .357 magnum revolvers only with our weak hands. We had no speed loaders at that time. Our extra ammo was kept in the old style loops worn on the gun belt. Using only the left hand, a right handed shooter would have to open the weapon's cylinder, stick the barrel inside the gun belt so that it would remain in place without being held, and then remove ammunition from the loops and load before firing with the weak hand.

The physical training was far more strenuous than anything at the NYPD academy. The length of most runs was three miles, and we had to be able to successfully navigate an obstacle course that included scaling two eight foot walls as well as climbing a twenty foot rope.

The other training that dwarfed the NYPD's program was driver training. If I remember correctly, NYPD recruits received a day or two at Floyd Bennet Field in Brooklyn where they had to successfully navigate through cones at a slow rate of speed. At FLETC we received 40-hours of training from Border Patrol driving instructors. We actually conducted high speed pursuits on a track designed for that purpose. An instructor in a tower would be in radio contact with the trainees. I can still remember one particularly intense instructor shouting in my radio "Get on it…Get on it" as he implored me to increase the speed of my pursuit. There also was a skid pan track where we could learn how to maintain control of the vehicle in controlled skidding situations.

The remaining training was only several hours at most in duration. The border patrol specific topics included:

- organization and function of INS
- officer's handbook
- forms and correspondence
- radio communications
- line watch
- remotely monitored sensors
- city scout

- farm and ranch check
- freight train inspection
- common carrier inspection
- sign cutting
- traffic check
- anti-smuggling program
- false claims to citizenship
- Alien Documentation Identification Telecommunications System
- Sources of information

The topics handled by the FLETC police training division instructors were:

- Latin American culture
- detention and arrest
- internal investigations
- orientation to federal law enforcement agencies
- typing
- effective writing
- interviewing
- human relations
- fingerprinting

- recognizing contraband narcotics
- civil disturbance orientation
- document frauds

Less than two years after I left the Border Patrol, I was appointed as a recruit in the New York City Transit Police Department. The police academy was serious business and I learned a lot. Frankly, however, I did not find the police academy particularly challenging. I believe this was at least in part due to the intense FLETC experience that made the police academy seem almost easy.

THE RODEO

Physical training consisted of some unique, and arguably ridiculous exercises. At some point, the instructional staff must have been tasked to create physical exercises that had a correlation to actual Border Patrol Agent duties – this one was a doozy. Whenever the instructors would terminate a run at the athletic field, we could always count on doing some good old fashioned "alien chasing." Fresh from a three mile jaunt, we would be directed into two lines. Line A were the aliens and Line B were the agents. At the instructor's whistle, the first person in Line A would take off running across the athletic field. Three seconds later the whistle would blow and the first person in Line B would take off running after the person already in flight. This was supposed to be a practical exercise for chasing aliens at the border. By the time a minute had transpired the field was filled with trainees running haphazardly in all directions. This exercise caused several injuries due to trainees running into each other, as well as several near-fights when pursuers would catch their prey and pull them to the ground with a bit more zeal than could be appreciated by the subdued party. This exercise also served as the platform for one of Steve's more humorous moments.

We had just completed a three mile run and jogged onto the athletic field for some alien chasing hijinks. I was fourth in line in the agent, or chaser line. Steve was directly in front of me and was sizing up who he would be chasing momentarily. Third in the alien line was Baxter Slocum. Baxter was a thirty-one year old from a small town somewhere in Northern California. Like just about everyone else in the class aside from Steve and me, Baxter had served in the military, and had been a police officer in his home town for the past couple of years.

Baxter was a nice enough guy, but he did everything slow, at least in the opinion of two guys used to the fast pace of New York City. He walked slowly, he talked slowly, and he even ate slowly in the mess hall. Baxter also had apparently let himself go a bit since his military days. He was six feet tall with a very noticeable paunch around his middle. At his optimum physical condition, I could not fathom Baxter being able to run fast, but with his ample midriff, he was a painfully slow runner.

After a quick assessment, Steve stated, "I'm gonna be chasing Baxter." He smirked and continued, "That's gonna be like a cowboy chasing a cow at a rodeo."

You could almost see the light bulb illuminate over Steve's head. He was at the front of the line as the whistle signaled Baxter to begin plodding ahead. Steve quickly turned toward me with a huge grin on his face. "Watch this."

The whistle sounded and Steve was off. As he almost instantly closed the distance with Baxter, he raised his right arm in the air and began turning his right hand in a circular motion. What the heck was he doing? He stayed about ten feet behind Baxter, and as I was in hot pursuit of my alien I passed in close proximity to Baxter and Steve. Being able to hear Steve's voice made it painfully clear what he was doing. As he ran behind Baxter with his hand waving in the air, he was shouting "YAHOO." Steve was pretending to be a cowboy in the act of lassoing a steer. When I realized what Steve was doing, I stopped momentarily, unable to continue my pursuit due to the fit of laughter that had overcome me. Baxter, on the other hand, did not find cowboy Steve in any way amusing.

GODS AMONG US

Greek mythology is a body of myths and teachings that belong to the ancient Greeks, concerning their gods and heroes, and the origins and significance of their own cult and ritual practices. It was part of the religion of ancient Greece. When I attended the Border Patrol Academy in 1978 I quickly learned that the Border Patrol had its own religion complete with two gods and heroes – Bill Jordan and Ab Taylor. From just about day one, every Border Patrol instructor would find time to pay homage to these two Border Patrol gods.

A couple of factors set the Border Patrol apart from other law enforcement agencies. First, the Border Patrol is the only agency that requires its officers to speak another language. The second factor unique to the Border Patrol is its rich tradition of sign-cutting. I quickly learned that sign cutting did not involve taking the proper saw blade to an actual sign, but instead involved the ability to track a person. No one was better at tracking than the Border Patrol. About a decade before I took the oath as an agent, the Border Patrol relied heavily on trackers or sign cutters in chasing down aliens illegally slipping across the nearly 2000 miles of Mexican border. As my class began its training, however, tracking had evolved into a luxury the border force could seldom afford. In the "Old Patrol" catching an alien out in the back country was a big deal. There could be as many as fifteen men tracking a case. But times changed.

In the late 1970s the number of aliens captured in a month had swollen to thousands from 10 to 20 a decade prior. In fact, as I began training during October, 1978, it was with the knowledge that nearly 300,000 apprehensions had been made during the first nine months of the year. The reality was that training in tracking was being de-emphasized. And why not? The sheer volume of illegal aliens was such that great groups of aliens were routinely caught. The Border Patrol could no longer afford the luxury of tracking a single alien. Seismic and infrared sensors had now become the tools of the hunt. Given the warnings of these sensors, agents could move in quickly to intercept lone crossers or vehicles full of them, rather than spending hours or days on the trail of a lone alien.

A manifestation of the move away from sign cutting as a realistic tool of apprehension was reflected in the academy curriculum. During the 16-weeks of training, sign cutting was covered in one two hour lecture and two field exercises for a total of six hours. Even so, I have to admit to a high degree of excitement waiting for the instructor to enter the classroom to begin the sign cutting lecture.

Agent Roger Dalton presented a unique appearance when he entered the room. Up to this point, every instructor, whether in Border Patrol or FLETC instructor uniform exhibited a military bearing with sharp, clean, crisp appearance. Agent Dalton looked like he had just woken up and had slept in his FLETC instructor uniform as he lumbered to the front of the classroom. He was tall and thin with a full head of uncombed sandy hair. He appeared to be in his mid-40s, but he never mentioned how long he had been with the Border Patrol. He smiled slightly as he commenced his very brief introduction.

"Mornin' fellas, this is sign cuttin'."

At some point he also mentioned that he was a Texan, which was obvious by his accent. Actually, maybe it wasn't really that obvious to someone sporting a thick New York City accent. To me, I guess the best way to describe his Texas accent was that he had a southern accent with a little "twist" to it.

Steve leaned close to me and whispered, "Look at this bumpkin. It looks like he just got back from tracking someone in the desert."

Have you ever heard someone talk on a subject you know nothing about, but you just know by the tone, pace and confidence of the person that he knows everything there is to know on the topic? That is the vibe I received from Agent Dalton. I was the guy whose first instinct was to think that sign cutting was actually cutting a sign with a saw, but even with my lack of knowledge, I was sure this man knew what he was talking about.

"There's always sign, boys"

With that simple statement he was off and running. I learned a lot during that two hour lecture, especially since I was starting with a knowledge base of zero. I learned that sign is the physical evidence of any disturbance of the environment left behind by animals, humans or objects, and that the detection of this sign is called sign cutting. Agent Dalton stated that a person cannot traverse ground without leaving some sort of telltale sign, and that this sign is what we're trying to find and track.

As I was trying to visualize being hot on the trail of an alien, the only sign I could envision was a footprint. Agent Dalton, however, stated that a trained tracker looks for more, such as kicked-over rocks, soil depressions, clothing fibers, changes in vegetation, and changes in the environment. I guess I was beginning to understand the message. The tracker looks for the disturbance — the sign — left behind by the person or persons being tracked. The sensors and cameras could be fooled, but as Agent Dalton pointed out – "The sign never lies."

It was during this lecture that I received my first initiation to a Border Patrol god. There were undoubtedly many great trackers throughout the history of the agency, but they were merely false gods. Agent Dalton was a disciple of Ab Taylor. This wasn't the first time I heard the name and it certainly wasn't the last, but this was like being told about Jesus directly from Saint Peter.

Ab Taylor was a plain-spoken Texan who became a legend in the art of man-tracking during his long career the U.S. Border Patrol. As he patrolled the rugged, unpopulated stretches of the U.S.-Mexico border, Taylor developed expertise in looking for the small signs — a broken twig, a small footprint, rocks out of place, patterns in the dust — that indicated the passage of immigrants trying to sneak into the United States. Dalton stated with pride that the more difficult the chase, the greater the satisfaction for Taylor. Dalton reflected on Taylor,

"Ol' Ab would always tell me that the tougher he is to beat, the more you admire him. If you catch him down there a mile away from the border and blunder into him, there certainly is no satisfaction there. But if Ol' Ab tracked him from sun-up one day to sundown the next … then he was satisfied in beatin' him."

The next day was the first of two sign cutting exercises. When Steve, Alan and I were about to exit our house to catch the bus to the mess hall and breakfast, Steve stopped us in the doorway. You may remember that I mentioned that we were not given access to the first floor of the house, and you also need to know that I had alerted Steve to my previous perception of what sign cutting was.

To keep us out of the first floor there was a gate across the entranceway to the living room. This 3-foot high gate was the type you would commonly see utilized to keep a toddler or a dog inside a specific room. Attached to this gate was a sign reading NO ADMITTANCE.

Steve nodded towards the gate while stating "I don't think we have to go today – we already passed."

I looked at the gate, and it took a few seconds to notice anything different. Then, it became clear. The NO ADMITTANCE sign had been cut in half. Steve could hardly stand up as we rushed for the arriving bus. His self-induced state of hilarity made it difficult for him to finish his punch line "We already cut sign – why do we have to go?"

I took my seat on the bus and tried to think about bacon and eggs. "Very funny, Steve."

The sign cutting exercise was extremely enlightening. I very quickly became enlightened to the fact that there was no way I was going to be able to use any of these techniques and actually find someone. The logistics of the exercises were quite simple. One instructor supervised a group of approximately eight trainees. Steve and I were assigned to Agent Dalton's group. The 1,600 acres of FLETC were mostly undeveloped woods, so it was very easy to produce an environment where groups would take turns being trackers and trackees. The instructor of the group being tracked would do everything possible to cover up the path of the group.

We spread out along the edges of a dirt road and began scanning for sign. I was excited and thrilled to be able to call out "Look, footprints!" I had discovered several sets of footprints that appeared to be leading off to the north. Agent Dalton squatted next to me and circled one of the prints with the edge of a stick he was carrying. "That's our group, son. But they ain't moving north."

I turned toward the instructor with a confused look on my face. Dalton motioned for the entire group to gather around while he continued to circle the footprint with his stick.

"The depression of a footprint can tell you a lot. It can tell you if the person is large or if he's carrying a heavy load. The dig tells us a lot too."

Steve whispered "What the hell is a dig?"

I just shook my head, hoping to get the answer from Agent Dalton.

"When all you have is half- moon shaped toe digs, then the person was running." Dalton poked his stick into the heel area of the print. "On this print, the dig is at the heel, indicating the person who made this print was walking backwards."

Agent Dalton looked at the group and smiled. "See how simple this stuff is."

Steve muttered under his breath, "If you say so."

Walking backwards? I should have realized right then and there that sign cutting was going to be a hopeless endeavor for me. As the exercises continued the situation only worsened. As we beat the brush looking for our elusive prey, some of my more rural brethren, which included everyone in the group except for Steve and myself, seemed to be getting the hang of it. We were hot on the trail of a group based on signs that I could have stared at for hours without noticing. Finally, the defining moment arrived when I realized all was lost. The group emerged from an area thick with trees and brush onto a dirt road. Our group studied the road while looking in both directions. Even the real country boys in the group were stumped. Agent Dalton began poking his stick around the dirt for a few seconds before declaring, "They crossed the road here."

"Huh."

Dalton explained "These boys actually did a pretty good job covering their tracks - but they forgot something that was a dead giveaway."

Steve and I exchanged glances. We couldn't wait for this one.

Agent Dalton crouched down and ran his stick along a 3-foot portion of the dirt road. "See these? They're dead giveaways and they missed them."

Some of the members of our group started to acknowledge the discovery, as there were several declarations of "Oh yeah" being murmured. Steve could control himself no longer. "Excuse me. What dead giveaway is everyone looking at because I don't see anything?"

Dalton looked up at Steve and calmly said, "Crushed rabbit turds, son"

Steve and I both sang out in a stereo of disbelief "Crushed rabbit turds?"

"Yes sir boys, these turds are crushed. Somebody walked over them. How could they have overlooked them?" Dalton shook his head and chuckled.
Steve looked at me, nodded his head and stated very nonchalantly, "Crushed rabbit turds." I returned the nod and the message. "Yes, crushed rabbit turds." The

message we had just exchanged was clear. There was absolutely no way that two trainee Border Patrol agents from New York City were ever going to be able to cut any sign, no less crushed rabbit turds. I might as well go find a saw and work on the remaining portion of the NO ADMITTANCE sign back at the house. I could certainly continue to worship Ab Taylor, but there was no way I would be able to emulate this Border Patrol god. Thank goodness I was going to a highway checkpoint station.

The Border Patrol was also fiercely proud of its firearms tradition – and rightfully so. At the time I joined the agency, the Border Patrol National Pistol team virtually owned every major shooting competition. While there were many great shooters in the Border Patrol, I quickly learned that there was only one real deity - Bill Jordan.

Bill Jordan was born in 1911 and served with the Border Patrol during some of the most violent years of the agency's history. With the outbreak of World War II he enlisted in the Marine Corps. After the war, he returned to duty with the Border Patrol until his retirement in 1965, after which became an exhibition shooter, famed author, firearms instructor and field representative for the NRA.

Jordan was famed for his fast draws and accurate hip shooting. One of his most popular fast-draw demos consisted of holding a ping pong ball on the back of his gun hand, with the palm hovering 6 inches above his holstered gun butt. Then, he'd move his hand, draw his revolver and fire, and the ball would be resting inside the holster, displacing the revolver after traveling less than a foot.

A staunch fan of the double-action revolver for police work, Jordan criticized the .38 Special as lacking the power to stop a violent criminal. Jordan's book, NO SECOND PLACE WINNER, is a tactical guide to surviving in a gunfight. If Bill Jordan was a border patrol god then NO SECOND PLACE WINNER was the bible. It was also due to Bill Jordan that my vocabulary expanded.

While training at the academy, several of the Border Patrol instructors used the expression "I'd ride the river with him" or "You wouldn't want to ride the river with him." The phrase was attributed to Bill Jordan and his book. It was used to complement or insult someone by indicating their reliability and trustworthiness. When Jordan worked in Texas he literally rode along the Rio Grande as it marked the boundary between the U.S. and Mexico. For men like Jordan, men whose livelihoods depended on being able to trust one's partner quite literally with their lives, it was no small thing to be considered good enough to ride the river with. Several years later I received the exact same message from police officers in New York City, but with a different term – Stand-up Guy.

There were many stories told to illustrate the god-like qualities of Bill Jordan. The tale that made the greatest impression on me involved a sheriff who was standing trial for murder for shooting and killing one of his own deputies.

The prosecution alleged it was a cold blooded killing while the sheriff contended he had caught the corrupt deputy in the middle of a drug deal, and that he had fired in self-defense when the deputy began to draw his weapon. The prosecution made a big issue over the sheriff's claim of self- defense and the fact that there was no evidence indicating the deputy was in the process of removing his gun from his holster. The sheriff's explanation was that he had been practicing his draws for decades, and had a lightning fast reaction time. The sheriff stated that as soon as the deputy made a move for his gun, he was able to draw, aim, and shoot, because he WAS that fast.

The prosecution scoffed at the sheriff's quick draw defense. Enter Bill Jordan. The sheriff's lawyer arranged a demonstration in the court to prove the sheriff's quick draw defense. Using a pair of revolvers inspected by the judge and jury, and then loaded with blank rounds, Jordan holstered his gun and handed the other to a deputy. He told the deputy to point the 2nd gun at him and shoot the instant he saw Jordan move. The deputy nodded, and Jordan went on talking for a moment, and then suddenly ripped his gun free and pulled the trigger literally before the stunned deputy had a chance to react. Jordan went back on the witness stand, and admitted that he was timed at being able to decide, draw, acquire, and shoot in a mere

0.27 seconds, compared with the normal human 1/2 second to merely recognize a threat. When asked about the abilities of the sheriff on trial, Jordan calmly stated, "Well, I reckon he's a mite bit faster'n me." The jury took just one hour to acquit the sheriff on all charges.

The Internet is an amazing research tool. Sometimes I take for granted how easy it is to unearth a wealth of information on just about any topic in a matter of seconds. To fully appreciate the wonder of this information age, all I have to do is think back to the 70s and 80s where information on some topics was sparse. My research on the Border Patrol prior to entering on duty was a prime example. I was able to find a single library book that referred to the Border Patrol as green devils. Today, I would need to travel no further than my computer key board to learn most anything about the agency.

Sometimes, however, the ability to retrieve data so quickly can result in finding blasphemous information. A few years ago I stumbled upon an Internet article regarding Bill Jordan. If this information was true- and I found numerous articles containing the same details – then this Border Patrol god was tainted. One of the articles read as follows:

At approximately 11:30 a.m., October 16, 1956, Patrol Inspector John A. Rector was accidentally shot by the firing of a .357 Magnum revolver by a fellow officer. The mishap occurred at the Chula Vista Sector Headquarters, where two officers were discussing various guns and their limitations and advantages. During the course of the conversation, the .357 Magnum was unloaded, examined, then reloaded, and placed in a desk drawer. The two officers then examined a .22 revolver and soon the discussion returned to the .357 Magnum. At this point, one of the officers reached into the desk drawer, picked up the pistol, and without realizing that it had been reloaded, pulled the trigger.

The bullet passed through a partition wall into Patrol Inspector Rector's office, where it struck him in the left jaw and ranged up through his head. Upon arrival of an ambulance and a doctor, Patrol Inspector Rector was removed to the Paradise Valley Hospital in National City. Two neurosurgeons from San Diego were called; however, nothing could be done for Inspector Rector. He died at approximately 2:00 p.m. the same day.

Every article I found identified that other officer as Bill Jordan. An accidental discharge can happen to anyone and it should not tarnish Bill Jordan's firearms abilities. Being a god, however, is synonymous to perfection. I want my gods to be infallible, and all these years later it was disappointing to find out that I was worshipping a god with the same human imperfections as you and me.

LA LLORONA

The academy curriculum included numerous law enforcement topics presented by the FLETC Police Training Division. Only one of these courses stands out in my memory – the four hours of training in Latin American culture.

Marco Zanetta was unique in several aspects. He was a member of FLETC's permanent instructional staff, but he had worked for five years as a Border Patrol Agent in the El Paso Sector before transferring to the Treasury Department. Zanetta originally hailed from Philadelphia, so his accent was closer to what I was accustomed to as opposed to the southern and western drawls I had heard from most of the Border Patrol instructional staff.

Zanetta appeared to be in his late thirties. He was average height and very thin. He had dark, deep set eyes with jet black hair that was slicked back. His complexion was very pale, giving him an overall ghoulish appearance – extremely appropriate for one of his covered topics.

It was obvious that Zanetta enjoyed relating the tale of La Llorona. All that was missing from his presentation was eerie organ music in the background. According to Zanetta, illegal aliens were not the only threats agents had to deal with on la frontera. Some of the threats, such as La Llorona, were supernatural in nature.

As usual, I was sitting next to Steve when Zanetta began his journey into the supernatural. He leaned into me and whispered, "Listen to this ghoul. He can't be serious."

"Ssshh," was my curt response. Like a kid sitting around a camp fire, I wanted to hear the ghost story.

According to Marco Zanetta the legend of La Llorona had been part of Latin American culture, particularly in the border region, since the days of the conquistadores. He said that no one really knew where the legend of La Llorona (Weeping Woman) began but that all the versions shared some common threads. Zanetta said that La Llorona was the spirit of a mother who had drowned her children, and that the spirit roams the rivers and creeks in the border region searching for her children. Zanetta continued to say that children living near rivers and creeks in the southwest are told not to go out at night out of fear that La Llorona, resplendent in a white gown, wailing for her lost children, will catch them and drown them. Zanetta seemed to be doing his best Bela Lugosi impression in saying that to this day, many PAs in the El Paso sector had claimed to have seen La Llorano wandering at night on the banks of the Rio Grande. Zanetta ended his presentation with a dramatic warning. "Beware the cries of La Llorona."

Marco Zanetta was done and you could have heard a pin drop in the classroom. Steve leaned in again to whisper, "This ghoul is obviously out of his mind."

During lunch, Steve had apparently reconsidered his mental assessment of Marco Zanetta. "There aren't any rivers on the border near Chula Vista, are there?"

Steve's concern was not immediately apparent. "I'm not sure Steve. I did some research on a map and I think the Tijuana River runs along the border for some distance, but nothing like the Rio Grande in Texas. Why the sudden interest in the Chula Vista border area?"

Steve looked at me like I had not studied material for a Spanish or Law test. "What's the matter with you? You didn't hear that guy this morning talking about that La Lunatic running around the border rivers drowning people?"

A small bit of burger inadvertently popped out of my mouth while I laughed. "Don't tell me you believed that guy?"

Steve rolled his eyes. "Let's just hope she's another one of these Texans that seem to be all over the place here."

"What?"

"Yeah, if she's a Texan, maybe she'll stay on the Rio Grande."

"You and the ghoul instructor are both out of your minds!"

Although I scoffed at Steve's trepidation regarding the spirit of La Llorona, I have to admit that I was glad to be going to San Clemente – sixty six miles north of the border. Now if only I could complete the academy without some other instructor telling tales of some hobgoblin terrorizing the highways of Southern California, I would be alright.

I have already commented on the differences in the Border Patrol Academy and the training I received and conducted in New York City. I suppose I will now have to add La Llorona to the list. In neither the New York City Police Academy nor the Transit Police Academy was there ever any subject matter warning the recruits of spirits roaming the streets and subways of New York City.

LINE WATCH

Without a doubt, the most anticipated academy class from the perspective of the trainees was the line watch exercise. This operation was conducted at night with about three weeks of academy training remaining. It was an opportunity for the trainees to go out in the field and utilize everything we had learned in performing the Border Patrol's most basic function – catching illegal aliens at the border.

After dinner, our class assembled in a classroom for a briefing about the exercise. We would be spread out in teams of two in a remote wooded area of FLETC that represented the international border. Members of the instructional staff would play the role of illegals trying to penetrate the border. Very simple parameters. Any illegals we apprehended would be transported via detention van back to our classroom/alien processing center where we would question and prepare the necessary paperwork for our detainees.

As seemed to be the case throughout most of the academy, I was teamed with Steve. Eight of us got into a van driven by Agent Dalton, our sign cutting instructor. We drove along a very dark dirt road for about five minutes. The only light was supplied by the van's headlights. This could have been the same area where we performed the sign cutting exercise, but in the darkness I could not tell. Frankly, it could have been broad daylight and I still probably would not have been able to identify the area. To me, one wooded area looked like another wooded area.

Every few hundred yards Agent Dalton would stop the van and a two man team would exit. Steve and I were the last team still in the van. Dalton pointed out the driver's window. "Your sector is about 50-yards off the road. Good luck boys."

Steve and I slowly made our way through the brush and trees with only our flashlights providing illumination. After a couple of minutes we broke out of the trees and into a clearing. The moon provided at least a minimum amount of light, and I could actually see Steve standing next to me. "I guess this is our sector."

As usual, Steve just could not agree or disagree. He had to provide commentary. "Ok. So which way is America and which way is Mexico?"

As entertaining as he could be, after thirteen weeks, Steve's act was becoming a bit stale. "Let's just assume that when people start appearing, they will be coming from Mexico, OK."

At the briefing, we were instructed that the exercise would begin at 8PM. It was now 7:45, so we still had about fifteen minutes before our alien hunt began. Suddenly, there was movement from the tree line. Steve whispered with an air of anticipation. "Here they come."

"No," I responded. "It's too early." Early or not, the shadow of a single figure came out of the trees. Our flashlights quickly revealed Bob Lorry, one of our classmates.

Lorry had used the prior 13-weeks of academy training to establish himself as being totally nuts. He hailed from Southern California and had the look of a 35-year old who had spent his entire youth surfing the Pacific Coast.

Lorry's surfer look was secondary, however. His most defining characteristic was his "Crazy Eyes." What are crazy eyes? In pointing out Lorry's lunacy, Frank Monte summed it up best. "Crazy eyes are when you can see white around the entire 360 degrees of the eyeball, and that lunatic Lorry has those crazy eyes."

Why Lorry was wandering around in the woods alone – I still don't know. His partner was probably happy that he had wandered off. In the glare of our flashlights, Lorry's eyes appeared even wider than usual. There was also something odd about his face other than his crazy eyes. His face was blackened with some type of paint. Before Steve or I could ask any questions, Lorry extended his hand and spoke in a very excited tone. "Here, put this on before the exercise starts."

With the aid of the flashlight, I could see that I was holding a jar of black camouflage face paint. Before I could get any further clarification Lorry was gone into the trees. Steve was first to respond. "This is ridiculous. We're going to be camouflaging our faces when we work on the border? What are we, some half-assed commandos?"

I certainly saw Steve's point, but I did not want to get into trouble. "I don't know, but I guess we ought to just do it." A few minutes later our new commando looks were complete.

It was now 8PM – exercise on. 8:05 – nothing. 8:10 – nothing. Every now and then we could hear the distant shouts of other teams who had obviously made contact – "Parate – Alce los manos!"

Finally, there was some movement at our tree line. Steve and I crouched in the darkness and silently waited to spring our trap. I could vaguely make out what appeared to be three shadows emerging from the trees. The shadows continued moving in our direction. I stood up and blocked their path, while lighting them up with my flashlight. "Halto!"

My perception of the shadows had been correct as three males were temporarily frozen in my beam. Their paralysis lasted for only a brief second when the male in the middle turned and began walking back towards the trees. "I said Halto." I shouted forgetting to use Spanish, except for one word.

Steve said nothing. There is an old saying that actions speak louder than words. If that saying is accurate then Steve may well have possessed a megaphone because his actions were at the highest volume. Without a word Steve trotted up behind the male walking towards the trees and grabbed him around the waist. What Steve did next I can only describe as being some type of wrestling suplex, as he lifted the male and slammed him to the ground face first, with Steve lying on top of him. The only sounds coming from the subdued male were shallow moans. The other two males, however, were quite vocal, and upset. Steve had just body slammed Joe Stanley, the chief officer at FLETC, and the two aides accompanying him were not happy.

Once Stanley had regained his wind and had been assisted to his feet, his aides were ready to turn their wrath toward Steve. They had just begun a chorus of *What the hell is wrong with you!* when Stanley cut them off. Thankfully for Steve, Stanley was apparently too embarrassed at being pulverized by a trainee to make an issue of it. For Stanley and his aides, however, the exercise was over as he limped off into the night with assistance. I turned toward Steve seeking some kind of explanation. "What the hell……"

Before I could finish my statement Steve cut me off. "Hey, for all I know that ghoul instructor conjured up that La Lunatic lady. How was I supposed to know?" I shook my head and said nothing. What kind of bizarre reality had I gotten myself into?

    Eventually, another group of illegals came our way, and we were able to take them into custody without further fanfare or assaults on the spirit world. Steve and I were the last team to return to the processing classroom. The room was a flurry of activity with the sound of Spanish interrogations and typewriters filling the air. The moment we entered the room all activity came to an abrupt halt. Everyone in the room, both trainees and instructors were focused on Steve and me. Most people were doing a poor job of holding in laughter. What the hell was going on?

Agent Bill Donovan, one of the lead instructors for our class came directly to us with a look of sheer disgust on his face. "Wipe that shit off you faces – now!"

In the space of a split second, I was trying to comprehend what was going on. No one else was wearing the camouflage face paint. Bob Lorry was off in the corner of the room with his usual crazy eye look, but wearing only remnants of face paint. Frank Monte walked up to me smiling and shaking his head. "I don't believe it. That lunatic actually found two guys as crazy as him."

I shot a look at Steve. He just shrugged his shoulders. "I told you the face paint was ridiculous."

NIGHTLIFE

New York City did not have to worry about losing its title of nightlife capital of the world to Glynco. The Border Patrol Academy was tiring both mentally and physically, but there were still many weekends where we strained to find something to do.

For those trainees looking to unwind with a drink on a Friday or Saturday night there were basically three options. Option number one was the club on the base. This was my preferred option. I could have a beer, listen to some live music, partake in some good conversation and then walk back to my house. Option two was a local bar that was so dependent on FLETC patronage that it provided van service between the bar and the base. Option three, and by far the least desirable option, was another local bar. The instructional staff warned us away from this establishment, characterizing it as a bucket of blood.

I did very little off duty socializing with my roommates. Steve usually stayed in his room all weekend. I partially admired his choice because he spent a lot of his weekend time studying Spanish, and this extra work was reflected in his high marks. The other reason he kept to himself, however, was that he always believed people were trying to bring him down. At least fifty times during the sixteen weeks of training Steve would declare, "Remember, trust no one!" Steve was particularly blunt in his assessment of our other roommate, Alan Wilson. Alan was a nice enough guy, but he was a bit of an odd duck. On most weekend evenings Alan would leave the base alone, returning just before sunrise completely inebriated. He would never say where he went or who he was with. On one Sunday afternoon, Steve and I were ready to leave for lunch at the mess hall. We had not heard a sound from Alan's room all morning, so we knocked on his door to see if he wanted to come eat with us. There was no response. Steve opened the door and we observed Alan sprawled naked on his bed, surrounded by at least twenty cans of tuna fish. Once we determined he was breathing we went on our way to lunch and left him with his tuna. We never asked and Alan never volunteered the back story to the tuna.

What bothered Steve most about Alan was his "Needy" nature. Alan always seemed to need something. Whether it was a pen, paper, a homework assignment, or a uniform item, Alan always seemed to be lacking something. What infuriated Steve the most, however, is when Alan would ask to borrow money, usually at the beginning of a weekend. Steve never loaned him any money, and on one occasion, he must have sensed me weakening to Alan's request, so he burst into my room to stop it. Steve declared that I was crazy if I gave this lamprey any money. After Alan had departed for his weekend activities without any financial support from me, I visited Steve in his room. As Usual he was studying Spanish. "What the hell is a lamprey?"

Steve closed the Spanish text book and turned to face me. "A lamprey is a parasitic fish that sucks the blood out of its prey." Steve pointed in the direction of Alan's bedroom door. "That guy is a lamprey. He will suck the blood out of you if you allow him."

"I get you point." I said while retreating back to my room. "Next time, try not to be so subtle." Well, at least I learned a new word.

Whether I was influenced by Steve's paranoid nature, or whether I was just exercising sensible caution, I never visited any of the off base bars. Even with this perceived common sense approach, I still ended up having an off base incident at a very unlikely location.

On a Saturday night about halfway through the academy training I decided to go off base for the evening with Rick Sanders. Rick was one of the trainees assigned to San Clemente who I had become friendly with. Rick said there was a roller skating rink about two miles south of the base. Roller skating? Oh well, why not? I had played roller hockey for years, so at least I would not make a fool of myself on the skates. When we arrived at the rink at about 8PM I was pleasantly surprised. It looked like a really nice family establishment and by the size of the crowd going in, it also appeared to be a popular night spot for the local population.

We entered the lobby of the rink to pay the entry fee and to rent skates. Almost immediately I could sense something was wrong. At first I thought too much of Steve had rubbed off on me because I had the feeling that several of the male employees were staring at me and talking about me. It also seemed to be taking way too long for the employee at the skate rental desk to bring Rick and me our skates. Finally, a rather large, middle age White male approached me. I immediately perceived this man to be the manager of the rink, as he was backed up by the several younger males who had been staring at me moments earlier.

The manager came right up to me and got in my face. "You got a lot of nerve coming back here."

"What?"

"After all the trouble you caused here last week."

"What are you talking about? I've never been here before."

The situation was escalating. I didn't appreciate this guy getting right up in my grill, so my primal instincts forced me throw out my chest in a ridiculous attempt at manly defiance. The trash talking went back and forth and was becoming more heated. Finally, I was grabbed by the shirt collar and unceremoniously yanked out the door of the rink. It wasn't the manager or any of his local goons who had given me the bum's rush. It was Rick.

Rick did not let go of me until we were a safe distance away from the rink. Rick gave me no chance to voice any protest. "Hey partner, think for a minute. We're in bulls prick, Georgia on a Saturday night, and worse yet, I'm with a New York City boy. You know how that ends, don't you? It ends up with me and you laying in some local jail cell with lumps all over our heads."

I got the point. We started the two mile trek back to base. We had only walked about fifty feet when I thought Rick was going to continue his reinstruction. "And you know what's most troubling?"

"What?" I said, not really in the mood to be given any more advice.

"What's most troubling is that there is someone else in this world who looks just like you." Rick slapped my back.

Oh well, I suppose I would have to admit that at least it was not another boring Saturday night in Georgia.

Rick and I had a lot in common. One of our shared interests was the Honeymooners television show. We would regularly bounce funny lines from the show off each other when the situation was appropriate. About halfway back to the base I suddenly realized that I was set up perfectly for a Honeymooners line. It was an episode where against his better judgement Ralph takes his wife Alice roller skating, resulting in disaster. I turned to Rick and said exactly what Ralph said to Alice in his same sarcastic tone. "You just had to go roller skating, didn't you?" .

I know, I know. Writers should stay away from funny stories that are too "inside" in nature. I don't know. I think there are enough Honeymooners fans in the world to make the line appropriate. If not, you're just going to have to take my word for it. It is a funny line!

STANDING ROOM ONLY

The sixteen weeks had flown by and the results were in. I had passed all the final exams in Spanish, Nationality Law, Immigration Law, Criminal Law, Human Relations, and several operational exams on FLETC police training topics. Additionally, I had passed the physical training, firearms training, and driver training. My overall average was in the high 80s – well above the 71 Badge & Gun standard.

Graduation day had finally arrived. The intense training was in the rear view mirror, and as I proudly strutted towards the FLETC auditorium in full dress uniform, a huge feeling of pride had overcome me. Of course I would still never really be able to track anyone, but I had passed all the written tests and qualified as an expert with the .357 magnum revolver.

The last graduation ceremony I had experienced was high school. Approximately nine months earlier when I was due to graduate college, it was suddenly brought to my attention that I was three credits short. I had completely forgotten that I had withdrawn from a class during my sophomore year. I never made that class up, and thus, I found myself just short of the finish line. It was not a big deal. I just had to take a class during the summer session. The school notified me that I could still be part of the graduation ceremony, but I declined. I refused to stand in cap and gown - throw the cap in the air and shout hip-hip hooray (or whatever it is that it vocalized), only to be seated in a new class a couple of days later. My parents weren't happy, but I was firm. No college graduation ceremony for me.

As my career progressed, I had the opportunity to be a part of numerous law enforcement ceremonies. There was my graduation from the NYC Transit Police Academy, followed by the ceremonies for my promotions to sergeant, lieutenant, and captain. Additionally, I spent several years as an instructor at the New York City Police Academy and was a part of several recruit graduations. My Border Patrol Academy graduation ceremony was very nice, and followed a similar script for all the succeeding ceremonies I was a part of.

The ceremony was held in the FLETC auditorium, which was a very nice building because it was very new. The stage, seating, and wood trim all had that very new, unused look. Throughout the sixteen weeks we had lost two classmates, so on this mild February Southern Georgia morning, thirty members sat proudly in the first two rows of the auditorium, ready to receive their US Border Patrol shields.

For two of the NYPD academy classes I was an instructor for, there were over two thousand students in each class. Graduation was held at Madison Square Garden, with the arena packed with family and friends as if it were and important Knicks or Rangers game.

I sat in silent anticipation in the first row of the auditorium as the dignitaries on the dais began to populate the stage. There were high ranking personnel from both the Border Patrol and FLETC, as well as all the FLETC and Border

Patrol instructional staff. Speeches commenced and awards were given to the class members with the highest academic, physical, and firearms scores. Next, the members of the graduating class were called to the stage one at a time to receive their shields and two graduation certificates. One certificate was for completion of the Border Patrol Academy and the other was for completion of FLETC's Police Training Division.

I was back in my seat with my precious loot safely in hand. I took a deep breath while the closing speech of a high ranking Border Patrol official provided background noise. I glanced around to try and savor the moment. As good as I felt I could not help but notice the very odd nature of this graduation ceremony. Surrounding the crowded dais and graduating agents was row after row of empty seats. The entire auditorium was empty. No one came to watch the graduation ceremony. In retrospect, I don't know why I found this peculiar. After all, I never expected my family to make the trip from New York City to Georgia for a one hour ceremony, and I guess the other families from all over the country felt the same way. Still, it was the first and only time in my life that I was part of a graduation or promotion ceremony that no one attended.

When the ceremony concluded there was very little time for glad handing and back slapping. I had a flight to catch in Jacksonville. Graduates were given a week's leave before having to report to their duty stations. I was flying direct to New York City for the week.

I probably should have gone straight to California and found someplace to live, but why waste time with something so inconsequential. I had a very simple plan. During the prior sixteen weeks I had become close friends with Rick Sanders, one of the other trainee agents assigned to San Clemente and my savior at the roller rink. Rick was a 26-year old Marine who was married with a two year old son. During the academy training Rick's wife and son had moved from Bakersfield, California into an apartment in San Clemente. Rick told me that there was a one bedroom apartment for rent across the street from his new apartment. I did not need to hear anything more. Without seeing photos, diagrams, or even getting a basic description of the place, I gave Rick the money to send to his wife so she could rent the apartment in my name.

With living arrangements taken care of my week in New York was basically a vacation. It also served as seven days for my parents, particularly my mother, to attempt to convince me to stay home in New York. Her pleas fell on deaf ears, but without telling anyone, I had made an important decision regarding my future. I really did miss my New York City home, family, and friends and I came to the conclusion that my future was going to be in New York. I was going to realize that future, however, on my own terms. I was not going to quit now and stay home like a homesick little kid. I was going to San Clemente and work for as long as it took for my own terms to develop. After a couple of years maybe I could transfer east to a job within the federal government. I could also see that the horrendous economic climate was showing some slight signs of improvement. There were bound to be civil service exams for police officer in NYC within a few years and I could always take that career path back home. For the time being, however, I was California bound. My immediate future was at San Clemente with the United States Border Patrol.

One note about how times have changed. When we graduated from the Border Patrol Academy, an instructor informed us of the process required to transport our newly issued firearms on our flights home and to our duty stations. There seemed to be an awful lot of paperwork and notifications. Too much work for my taste. I simply stuffed my 357 magnum revolver into a carry-on bag and brought it with me on both my flights from Jacksonville to NYC and from NYC to California. How times have changed. Imagine trying to bring an unreported firearm onto a plane today in your carry-on bags.

THE SIGN

In 1995 I was a lieutenant with the New York City Police Department, fifteen years removed from my Border Patrol experience. I was in the midst of a rare evening at home. With a 5-year old girl and a 2-year old boy usually running wild in the house, this was indeed one of those extremely unique evenings where peace and quiet seemed to be winning the night. Attempting to take full advantage of the opportunity I scanned through the channels of cable television confident of finding something of interest. Hundreds of channels available, yet I could find nothing. This was not the first time I failed to find an island of satisfaction among an ocean of television channels, so I always had a default plan. When all else failed, there was always something at least mildly interesting on the Discovery Channel. I eased back in the sofa, and with a tap of the remote control I was transported to Discovery. I instantly shot forward to the edge of the sofa because

Discovery had just transported me back in time fifteen years.

The show was a documentary about a simple road sign. In the early 1990s, the California Department of Transportation had been tasked with creating a road sign to alert drivers to a possible danger. This danger was not a sharp curve, slippery road, or falling rock area. Silhouetted against a yellow background and the word "CAUTION," the sign featured a father, waist bent, head down, running hard. Behind him, a mother in a knee-length dress pulls on the slight wrist of a girl — her pigtails flying, her feet barely touching the ground.

Caltrans (California Department of Transportation) installed ten such signs along Interstate 5, north of the Mexican border. They became iconic markers of the perils of the immigrant journey north. I immediately flashed back to the San Clemente checkpoint.

The checkpoint was the last barrier faced by illegal aliens on their way to Los Angeles. 66 miles north of the Mexican border and several miles south of the city of San Clemente, the United States Border Patrol conducted interior immigration enforcement on the San Diego Freeway.

When the average person thinks of the Border Patrol in today's environment of promises to build a border wall, the vision usually fashioned in one of agents on the border line gazing south into Mexico, maybe across the Rio Grande. A major operational segment of the Border Patrol, however, takes place nowhere near the border.

Permanent immigration checkpoints have been critical to Border Patrol operations and are relied upon as a second line of defense beyond the actual border.

The Border Patrol's responsibilities on the southern border span nearly 2,000 miles, from the shores of the Pacific Ocean in San Diego, California to the banks of the Rio Grande in Brownsville, Texas. However, the Border Patrol's actual authority – stemming from old case law and even older statutes – extends as far as 100-miles inland from all points of the geographic perimeter. Checkpoints positioned there, deep within the interior of the country, are credited as

integral components in what the Border Patrol refers to as its "layered
approach" to protecting the country. Though seemingly counterintuitive
to Fourth Amendment principles, the checkpoint's immigration control objective has withstood years of community opposition, constitutional scrutiny, and court challenges.

The operational concept of the San Clemente checkpoint was quite simple. With the aid of orange traffic cones, the four northbound lanes of the San Diego Freeway were shrunk to two lanes. A portable stop sign affixed to a four foot pole sat on the lane marking separating the two open lanes. Two huge highway signs dominated the space above the stop sign. The signs were electronically controlled and when in the "OPEN" position, approaching vehicles could not help but see flashing amber lights drawing attention to the sign's message of STOP HERE U.S. OFFICERS. When the checkpoint was not in operation and the cones and stop sign were not in place, the signs were put in the "CLOSED" position. To passing motorists the closed signs appeared to be nothing more than blank highway signs.

Posted precariously behind the stop sign was a Border Patrol Agent. This was the point man and was one of the three positions required to run the checkpoint. The point man made the first observations of vehicles passing in both lanes. When something about the vehicle or the occupants was suspicious, the vehicle was directed to the east shoulder of the road for secondary inspection. The two agents in secondary comprised the remainder of the three-man checkpoint team. The secondary agents conducted a thorough inspection of the vehicle and occupants. Although there were other activities taking place in the areas surrounding the freeway, this highway checkpoint was the primary station activity I became a part of.

When I worked at San Clemente, the Border Patrol's mission was limited in its scope to enforcing only the immigration laws of the United States. At the checkpoint, inspections were looking for one thing and one thing only – illegal aliens. If other contraband, such as drugs were discovered, these seizures were always the secondary result of an immigration inspection. Believe me, there were a lot of drugs seized at that checkpoint. On paper, however, The Border Patrol at the San Clemente checkpoint made no drug seizures. All the drugs were turned over to the Drug Enforcement Administration and became a statistic for DEA. Years later I was assigned to the Narcotics Division of the NYPD. There were times during street buy & bust operations when pickings were slim and the team would have to settle for arrests of several individuals observed carrying joints behind their ears. It was at times such as these that I would recall the commonplace occurrence of discovering bales of marijuana in vehicles at the San Clemente checkpoint and thinking that it was no big deal.

There were also activities involved with opening and closing the checkpoint that could be just as dangerous as working the point. "Throwing Up" and "Tearing Down" the checkpoint involved placing and removing the traffic cones from the highway. Beginning about a half mile south of the point, small paint marks had been made on the highway to denote the locations where traffic cones should be placed to gradually transition from four lane to two lanes.

Two Border Patrol vehicles were an integral part of the checkpoint set up. One was an older Ram Charger that had a wood platform installed across the rear fender. A vertical piece of pipe was attached to this platform to serve as a location to stack the traffic cones. The other vehicle looked like an old bread truck. In this vehicle the cones were stacked next to the driver.

When the order was given to "Throw Up" the checkpoint, four agents would man the two vehicles. There were two drivers and two cone setters. The drivers would take their respective vehicles south along the east and west shoulders of the northbound lanes until reaching the starting point for the cones. They would then start driving north while the cone setters placed the traffic cones on the paint marks. Being a newbie at the station I was always a cone setter. For a cone setter the more desirable vehicle was the bread truck where the setter crouched next to the open passenger door, reaching behind every few seconds for a new cone to place. The wood platform on the rear of the Ram Charger was the more dangerous cone setting assignment. The cone setter sat on the platform with his legs dangling over highway. As the Ram Charger drove north the setter would keep reaching to his left to grab a cone off the stack and place it on a paint mark. The wood platform was a very rough ride. One bad bump and the cone setter could be planted on the highway.

Further enhancing the dangerous nature of this activity on a major highway was the *Boys will be Boys* attitude by some of the agents. Cone setting races were commonplace with the bread truck and Ram Charger tooling up the east and west sides of the freeway at over twenty miles per hour. I hope I don't sound conceited, but I became expert at the art of high speed cone setting. The technique was the same for either side of the highway, but I found it more difficult on the back of the Ram Charger because I was facing the opposite direction as I set the cones. The trick was to hold the cone at an approximate two o'clock position and release it far enough behind the paint mark so that it would remain upright and slide into place over the mark. If a cone fell over, the vehicle had to stop and the cone setter had to jump off the vehicle and pick up the cone. There were many skills that I picked up in the Border Patrol that were helpful in my subsequent New York City police career. It was a shame, however, that cone setting, my top skill acquisition, was never of use again.

Commencing checkpoint operations resulted in a chain reaction for the illegal traffic already traveling north on the freeway. To avoid capture, smugglers would drop off their passengers at the shoulder of the highway or on the median strip just south of the checkpoint. They would then drive through the checkpoint while smiling politely and waving to the agent behind the stop sign. Five minutes later the smuggler was parked somewhere in San Clemente, enjoying a cup of coffee while waiting for his load to rejoin him.

To avoid the checkpoint, the aliens who suddenly found themselves without a ride, had two choices. They could try to pass the checkpoint on the east, but that route involved facing a range of hills and patrols from the adjacent Camp Pendelton Marine Corps Base. The alternative, which seemed on face value to be the much better choice, was to move to the west and walk north along the San Onofre Beach. The problem with the westward movement, however, was that they would have to cross up to eight lanes of traffic to get to the west side of the highway and the beach. This was not an attempt to trot across a country road - this was the San Diego Freeway. Combine the volume and speed of the traffic along with that fact that many of the illegals came from rural areas with little understanding of the danger and the result was a recipe for disaster.

Unfortunately, it was an all too common occurrence for aliens to be struck by speeding freeway traffic while attempting to sprint across the highway. According to the Discovery show, after I left the Border Patrol in 1980, the wild conditions of people sprinting all over the freeway had only worsened throughout the 1980s and 90s. The area near the checkpoint had become the scene of much carnage because of a cat-and-mouse game involving the smugglers and agents at the checkpoint. In fact, during the 1980s, more than 100 people were killed as they tried to cross freeway lanes between San Clemente and Oceanside. Caltrans wanted to do something about the problem and asked a California Department of Transportation employee to come up with a sign that would alert drivers and could reduce the number of deaths.

Caltrans eventually settled on using the image of a family in an effort to tug at the heart in a way a typical road sign might not. A little girl with pigtails, they thought, would convey the idea of motion, of running. Caltrans first installed the signs in late 1990 and early 1991. After workers erected a median fence along the freeway's trouble spots in 1994, officials decided not to replace any future signs that were lost. Around that time, federal officials launched Operation Gatekeeper, which fenced off the U.S.-Mexico border in San Diego — pushing illegal immigration east, toward Arizona and Texas. That helped reduce the number of freeway-crossing deaths, Caltrans officials said.

    The expert on this television show was not a Border Patrol Agent from the San Clemente station. Rather, a member of the California Highway Patrol provided commentary throughout the show. This CHP officer stated that most of the freeway sprints were made at night, with most accidents occurring between 8 P.M. and midnight. He said that compounding the problem was the fact that the illegal aliens usually cross in groups of people, rather than one or two at a time and that they are often holding hands. The officer shook his head in summing up the chaos by saying that the illegals are disoriented and tired as they attempt to cross eight lanes of freeway traffic.

The show did not really comment on the impact of the signs. Instead, it talked about the extinction of them. Slowly but surely they began to disappear — victims of crashes, storms, vandalism and the fame conferred on them by popular culture. As I watched this show in 1995, only one sign remained, and when it was gone, it would not be replaced — the result of California's diminished role as a crossing point for immigrants striving to make it to America.

Seeing the show on that sign brought back many memories of my time at the Border Patrol checkpoint in San Clemente – some good – some not so good. The triumphs, the tragedies, the laughter, and the outright craziness crammed into less than two years. In retrospect, the action I experienced as a Border Patrol Agent occurred as rapidly as the traffic on the San Diego Freeway.

But what of that sign that brought back such vivid memories. The show recounted how a generation after they were installed, the last of the "running immigrants" signs stood on two wooden posts in a concrete median of northbound Interstate 5, just before a "Welcome to California" sign. The view of the sign showed remnants of a broken taillight, a tattered ice cream wrapper and a couple of resilient weeds speckling the ground around it. Cars and trucks whizzed by on the windy freeway. Motorists quickly accelerated after hours of waiting in congested traffic to cross into the United States.

The Caltrans employee who designed the sign still lived in San Diego. In the final scene of the show, the employee visited the last sign with his son. After snapping some photos he turned to his son and said, "It served its purpose."

C&Es

When I arrived at the San Clemente Border Patrol station I had a single goal – to successfully complete probation and remove the "Trainee" status from my life forever.

To erase that hideous (t) required every time I wrote my title, I had to successfully complete the one year probation period. To complete the probationary period I first had to successfully complete the academy. After the academy, I had the chance to get my feet wet at San Clemente for about a month and a half, before it was down to the Chula Vista Sector for the five and a half month test. This was a written test on immigration law and Spanish, but if my recollections are correct, this was not a one and done test. You could fail this test and still survive for another day. That other day came several months later in the form of the ten month exam. It had been drilled into my head since day one at the academy that the ten month test was the whole ball of wax – the big enchilada. Fail the ten month exam and you're out. I believe there was a written component to the test, but by far the most important section of the exam was the oral Spanish test. Each trainee met with a sector chief one on one to carry out a lengthy conversation in Spanish. The trainee assumed the role of the agent while the chief played the alien. There was a long interrogation that included informing the alien of his Miranda Rights.

The rumor prevalent among the trainees was if the powers that be wanted to keep you, the chief would go easy on the test, but if you were persona non grata, the test would be brutal. What was it that made a trainee desirable or undesirable at the time he sat for the oral test? The answer to the question could be found in two letters – C and E.

After completing academy training, trainees at their duty stations received field training from Border Patrol Agents and supervisors who were required to complete Conduct and Efficiency (C & E) evaluations for each trainee. The C & E evaluations were recorded on a standard two-page form containing various categories that the evaluator used to rate the trainee. The evaluator also had to make a recommendation either for or against retention of the trainee. I don't remember the exact number, but I do remember receiving a C&E every few weeks.

Just before the ten month exam the trainee met with the station chief for his evaluation – a sort of super C&E. After the ten month exam, a Probationary Review Board made a recommendation for retention or non-retention based on the trainee's C & E evaluations, the station chief's recommendation and grades on the ten month exam. The Probationary Review Board's recommendation was forwarded to the Sector office and then to the Region office, which made the final decision of retention or non-retention. In reality, the trainees were told that they would be informed by the sector chief at the completion of the ten month test whether they had passed and would successfully complete probation. The other big rumor was that failure to obtain a recommendation for retention from the station chief was the kiss of death.

My first few months at San Clemente progressed well. I was learning the job every day and the supervisors and veteran agents seemed to be happy with me. Additionally, I passed the five and a half month exam with very good marks and every couple of weeks I received a glowing C&E from either a supervisor or a veteran agent. All was right with the world. Or so I thought.

The final hurdle to completing probation was the ten month exam, and at approximately the eight month mark, something happened. To this day I do not know what it was – but it was definitely something. My first clue of a problem occurred at the end of a day shift. The agents mailboxes were directly adjacent to the rear exit of the station – the same exit used to access the parking lot. It was a very common practice for me to give a quick look into my mail box as I was on my way out the door to go home. On this day, the quick scan of my mailbox revealed something inside. I grabbed the paper and continued to my car. I got into my car, started the engine, and then examined the document. It was a C&E completed by a supervisor who had previously completed several other C&Es on me. Nothing unusual, except this C&E was marked BELOW AVERAGE and NOT RECOMMENDED FOR RETENTION. I sat in my car for several minutes with the engine idling. I was stunned. I should have turned off the engine and returned to the station. The supervisor who prepared this C&E was still inside and I should have asked for a meeting to determine where my performance had suddenly become substandard.

But I did not address the C&E immediately. Instead, I went home and stewed about it over a pizza, reconciling that it was some kind of anomaly. I quickly put the C&E behind me.

Life at the station returned to normal. I never said anything about the C&E to the supervisor and he never addressed it with me. Maybe I was right. It had just been an isolated bump in the road. The bump, however, turned into a mountain. Another negative C&E from a different supervisor materialized. Again, I said nothing, and again, the preparing supervisor did not address me personally. Several more negative C&E's followed, and as the ten month exam approached, the icing on the cake occurred when a veteran agent who was not even scheduled to prepare a C&E on me, submitted a negative C&E. As ridiculous as this sounds, I still remained silent. I didn't know what to think or do. Of course I talked about it with a few of the agents who I was friendly with. I wanted them to tell me honestly if there had been anything about my performance that had declined over the previous several weeks. It was actually disappointing that no one could point out an obvious deficiency. If I knew I was doing something wrong, I could take action to correct it. Of course I just could have asked the people who prepared the negative C&Es for an explanation, but this was me being Stunod, or stupid (more about Stunod later).

What was most troubling was the more sinister theory being espoused by my friends at the station. More than one friendly voice stated that I had three factors working against me. First, I was the youngest agent at the station. Second, I had not served in the military, and finally, I was from New York City. When looking at the names of the negative C&E authors, my allies stated that they were not surprised by a bias against a kid who had not been in the military. All my friends were consistent in their opinion that the biggest alienating factor about me was my New York City heritage. I found this theory astounding. Having resided nowhere else but NYC, it never occurred to me that there could be a strong bias against New Yorkers from people hailing from other parts of the country.

Before I continue with this sad story, let me be very clear about something. I don't want this to sound like a case of sour grapes on my part, and that there must have been some other explanation for these negative evaluations besides poor performance on my part. I realize that I was not a perfect Border Patrol Agent and I am sure there were many areas I could have improved. Maybe these supervisors and veteran agents were being sincere in their negative assessments of my performance. Still, it was very peculiar that with the flip of a switch I went from all great C&Es to all negative reports. Stanger still was the fact that no one approached me to talk about the substandard performance. The only indication was a report in my mailbox. Again, I am predominantly to blame here. I should have addressed these reports personally with each evaluator – but I didn't

Whether it was bias, my performance, or a combination of factors, my allies kept insisting that all was not lost. They all said that the C&Es were minimal in importance, but that the "super" C&E prepared by the station chief was the evaluation that counted. There seemed to be universal agreement that as went the chief's recommendation, so went the career. In other words, if the chief recommended retention, you were in, but if the chief recommended that you not be retained, you were done.

The handshake and welcome aboard I had received after graduating from the academy was still the only interaction I had with the chief. Ten days before the ten month exam was scheduled. I had my personal interview with the chief. At the end of this interview he would give me my make or break C&E.

Patrol Agent in Charge John Wallace was tall, rugged-looking Texan. Looking back, I should have had the insight to consider this strike one since all my other negative C&Es were penned by Texans. Strike two was clear enough when the chief refrained from making eye contact throughout the interview. Strike three was a forgone conclusion. Part of the interview involved maintaining a brief Spanish dialogue with the chief. I can say in all humility that my Spanish was good. I received good marks in the academy and I was improving daily through use at work. The fact of the matter was that my Spanish was as good, if not better than any "Gringo" agent. It was also obvious during my brief conversation with the chief that his Spanish was horrible.

At the completion of the dialogue, the chief picked up a piece of paper that was in front of him on his desk. He held it up momentarily while delivering his assessment. "It's obvious that your Spanish is very deficient."

As he reached to hand me the paper I was wondering if this was some type of joke. My Spanish was deficient? His was terrible and he was the chief of the entire station. The paper I was now holding was the completed C&E. My eyes darted towards the bottom of the page and the chief's recommendation. I gulped. A big, black X was inserted in the box adjacent to NOT RECOMMENDED FOR RETENTION. The war was over and I had lost. I was stunned. Apparently, the proficiency of my Spanish had no relevance, seeing as the non-retention box was checked before the Spanish conversation took place.

Fifteen minutes later I was back on the side of the highway working in secondary. I was still stunned. What was I going to do? Should I play out the charade by staying until the ten month exam, only to be given my walking papers, or should I quit right now and save myself further embarrassment. What was distressing me the most was the embarrassment I would encounter 3000 mile away with a humiliating return to New York City. Even after I had made the decision to eventually return to NYC, I vowed to return under my own terms. Time and again I pledged that I would never just quit the Border Patrol and go crawling back to mommy and daddy, a kid who just couldn't cut it on his own. I wanted to go home, but I would only leave for another job, whether it was a transfer within the federal government or a job with a City or State agency. I never ever considered an alternate scenario in which I was subject to a humiliating return via termination. But here I was, dazed and confused in secondary with the prospect of being terminated staring at me in ten days.

Joe Conners was with me in secondary during my time of crisis. Joe was not one of my small circle of allies, but he was a good guy. Joe was from the Denver area, and with a little more than twelve years on the job, he was one of the most senior agents at San Clemente. It was no secret that the trainees at San Clemente were being scheduled for their interviews with the chief, so it was quite natural for Joe to say "How'd it go?" I suppose my glassy eyes were all the answer that was required, as Joe followed with "Not good, huh?"

I just shook my head and stared at the cars rolling north on the freeway. After a few seconds of uncomfortable silence Joe continued. "So what are you gonna do?"

I shrugged "I don't know. As soon as I get off the point I might just go inside and quit and be done with it."

Another moment of silence until Joe chimed in with words that changed my immediate course. "Why do you want to make it easy for them?"

I looked at Joe for clarification. "What do you mean?"

"Whether you deserve it or not, it's obvious that there are people here that don't want you around anymore."

My look of confusion alerted Joe that he needed to continue. "Why are you going to make their job easy by quitting?"

"What alternative do I have?"

Joe sounded a bit annoyed. I don't know whether it was at me or the contingent looking to jettison me. "I'll tell you what alternative you have. You can spend the next ten days doing nothing but studying for the exam. Make your Spanish so good that it will be an effort to get rid of you. You go in there with near perfect Spanish and at least you'll know it was a hit job if they still get rid of you."

Joe's words were not an epiphany. When I went off duty that day I sat in my car for a few minutes, seriously contemplating whether I would return and resign. Instead, I visited the Carl's Jr. drive thru window and brought home a Superstar with cheese and some fries for supper. I ate my burger, watched TV, feeling very sorry for myself. Sometime during an episode of One Day at a Time, the epiphany struck. Joe was absolutely right. Why should I help the chief and his band of shit kickers. If they wanted me gone, they would not be able to use the ten month exam as an excuse.

For the next ten days every waking moment was spent buried in my Spanish books. When the day of the exam finally arrived, I was as prepared as I possibly could be. The night before I had completely packed. I was still being a realist, and if I failed, I was not going to stretch out the exercise in futility any longer. The exam was conducted at the Chula Vista sector, and my plan was to return to San Clemente, resign, and be on a flight to New York City the next morning. What was concerning me on the morning of the exam, however, was having to spend the whole day with my academy classmates. Including me, there were a total of five of us going to Chula Vista to be tested. I was the only trainee who had received a recommendation not to be retained from the chief, so I assumed that everyone would be in a festive mood during the post exam ride back to San Clemente. Everyone except me, that is.

At approximately 7 AM I gathered with Frank Monte, Rick Sanders, Bob "Crazy Eyes" Lorry, and Baxter Slocum in the administrative room of the station. Frank obtained a set of keys for one of the station's vehicles and said "Let's go."

About an hour later we were at the Chula Vista sector. My memory is not totally clear on this, and I don't have any documents to back this up, but I believe there was a written law section of the test that we all took together. This was basically a pass/fail test that was the preliminary to the big oral Spanish exercise. Once the law test was completed, we were taken one at a time for our Spanish exams. Frank was the first to go while the rest of us waited at the same picnic tables where we had assembled ten months earlier on our first day.

The sector chiefs offices were in a separate building located on a small hill about fifty yards from the picnic tables. We had been given our order of testing and the rule of the day was for the next trainee up to proceed to the chiefs building when the prior trainee returned from the exam. There was not much small talk at the picnic table. Obviously, we were all nervous.

Rick was the first to see him on the path "There's Frank, you're up."

I took a deep breath and stood up, shaking hands with Rick, Bob, and Baxter while receiving their well wishes. As I approached Frank on the path he smiled and gave a thumbs up sign. "I passed." He stated as we shook hands.

"Congratulations, Frank." I stated as we released hands and I continued my path up the hill.

I had taken three or four steps toward my fate when Frank called out, "Hey Devo," he shouted, using the ridiculous nickname he coined for me in the academy, "You can do this!"

I responded with a weak smile and a half-hearted thumbs up before continuing the journey to my probable extinction. Frank was one of my staunchest allies and he knew the situation. I really appreciated his support.

Five minutes later I was seated on one side of a large, well-worn wood desk, nervously facing Chief Don Gardner. I knew absolutely nothing about Chief Gardner, but upon hearing that Texas accent that I had become all too familiar with, my low spirits sank further, if that was possible.

After all the stress from the C&Es and the studying, it was on. Chief Gardner was the illegal alien and I, possibly for the last time, was the Border Patrol Agent. I read him his rights in Spanish and conducted a complete and comprehensive interrogation. I covered all his pedigree information including where he was from and the names of all his relatives. I determined where he had crossed the border and how much he had paid a smuggler. The conversation went on for about thirty minutes and at completion, I knew I had nailed it. There was no feeling of elation, however, because my experience with the station chief at San Clemente was still a fresh wound.

Chief Gardner sat back and silently stroked his chin with his right hand. He was studying a file folder that was open in front of him. I took a deep breath and prepared myself for the inevitable. He was obviously reviewing my file containing the negative C&Es. He closed the file and leaned back in his chair. I was holding my breath as the chief spoke. "It looks like you had a few problems in recent weeks."

I never considered that I would receive any opportunity to offer an explanation for the negative evaluations, so I had to think fast. I did know that the worst thing I could do was attempt to portray myself as a victim, so my response sounded something like this. "You are right sir. I have experienced some problems recently. I am not exactly clear on what I was doing wrong, but I realize that I have been deficient, and I am doing everything in my power to correct these deficiencies."

As soon as the words exited my mouth I wished I could take some of them back. I was trying not to play the victim, but how could I say that I was trying to correct some phantom deficiencies. Hadn't I asked what the problems were? Remarkably, there was no follow up questioning – just a statement.

Chief Gardner said, "Well, your Spanish is impeccable and I'm glad you're taking corrective steps. Congratulations Agent Bryan."

It took a couple of seconds for me to meet his extended hand. I was once again stunned, but for the first time in a positive way. It was over and I had made it. I could have floated down that hill to the picnic table. I embraced Rick halfway down the path and wished him good luck. I received congratulations from Baxter, Bob and Frank, but quickly excused myself from the picnic table. I made my way to the nearby pay phone and made a collect call to NYC. I had briefed both my parents on the real possibility of my return, so it was obvious that my mom did not share in my elation that I would be remaining in California.

The ride back to San Clemente was not the party I had anticipated. Baxter Slocum had failed the exam and was now faced with the reality of imminent termination that I believed had been reserved for me. The exam results had already been phoned ahead to San Clemente, so when we arrived at the station, congratulation and well wishes seemed to be coming to Frank, Rick, Bob and myself from all angles.

The moment of extreme irony occurred when I was walking across the parking lot to my car. Getting out of a Border Patrol sedan was Agent Carl Hanson. Carl called out to me and approached with a huge grin and an extended hand. As we shook hands I could not help but appreciate the irony. Carl was the veteran agent who had prepared the negative C&E that was not even scheduled. As quiet and non-confrontational as I had been throughout the whole ordeal, I realized that I had to say something.

"Looks like you're stuck with me, Carl."

"Oh, don't say that." Carl responded while feigning astonishment.

I got in my car and headed north. I don't think I had ever felt better since arriving at the station. I was still determined to go home to NYC, but now it was going to be under my terms. For the moment all was right with the world. What the hell, I would have two Superstars with cheese at Carl's Jr.

NORTH

For most illegal aliens the perilous journey across the border was only half of the battle. Of course there were some illegals who crossed almost daily to work in farms and ranches within approximately fifty miles of the border. For these undocumented workers the Border Patrol sometimes served as a commuter service, facilitating their trip home after a hard day at work. For the majority of illegals, whose aspirations were well beyond the border country, the trip north had to be negotiated. That northern sojourn usually terminated in Los Angeles, with LA being the final destination or the jumping off point for continuing journeys all over the country.

For those illegals who were successful in crossing the border near the San Ysidro port of entry, the trip north meant dealing with the Border Patrol again at interior checkpoints. There was a checkpoint on Highway 15 at Temecula, and I was part of the welcome wagon waiting on the San Diego freeway near San Clemente.

Smuggling operations were like travel agencies, with different packages for different prices. For those on a very tight budget there was simply the trip across the border from Tijuana into America, where the client was on his own. Those travelers with a little more to spend would receive transport across the border as well as a trip to Los Angeles. The deluxe packages included additional travel from LA to destinations like Chicago or New York. When I was working the checkpoint in 1980 the going rate for a package that included a trip across the border to Los Angeles was about $200. I can only imagine what such a trip would cost today.

For the illegals travelling north via I-5, there were three methods for dealing with the San Clemente checkpoint. First, they could blow through the checkpoint and simply try to outrun the Border Patrol during a high speed pursuit. Believe me, there were enough of these pursuits, but thankfully, this method seemed to be the choice for the overwhelming minority of northern seeking illegals.

My personal opinion was that few, if any of these checkpoint runners actually formulated a plan in which they would attempt to outrun the Border Patrol. I believe that most of these individuals didn't do their homework and did not know of the existence of the checkpoint, or thought they would be passing through at a time the checkpoint was not operating. Others simply believed they would be able to drive through the checkpoint unchallenged. Either way, once under Border Patrol scrutiny, I believe most of these drivers panicked, initiating the pursuit.

The second way to defeat the checkpoint was to avoid it. This very common method involved temporarily giving up the luxurious accommodations inside the trunk of a car in order to walk around the checkpoint, either on the beach or inside Camp Pendelton. Those fortunate enough to avoid detection while walking around the checkpoint were picked up somewhere north of the checkpoint, and the trip north continued.

The final and most basic method of evasion involved simply fooling the Border Patrol agents at the checkpoint. Fooling the agent at the point involved trying to look totally natural and unconcerned while passing. The easiest way for a driver to be directed into secondary was to be "Hinky." Being hinky was a form of fear induced paralysis where the driver and or passengers maintained a fixed, wide eyed stare straight ahead, even when being questioned. There were other signs I quickly learned to look for while on the point.

Incongruities when questioning a nervous driver, like a single key in the ignition was sometimes a sign of a vehicle being used for smuggling. Think about it. Even today, most people that still use a physical car key keep that key on a chain with house keys, work keys, and all other manner of knickknacks. Another sign was a car riding low in that back – a sign of a heavy load in the truck - maybe people.

In the almost two years I worked that checkpoint, I saw illegal aliens hide in the trunks of cars, stacked in the beds of pickup trucks and covered with tarps and locked inside toolboxes in the bed of a pickup truck. I also saw aliens secreted behind the dashboard and in the engine block, although to this day I still have no idea how they managed to get into these tight areas.

The trunk was the indisputable workhorse of alien hiding places. The rule of the checkpoint was that every vehicle directed to secondary had to open the trunk for inspection. Agents working secondary could not release that vehicle until the interior of the trunk was inspected. Once in a while, that would lead to some complicated situations. This was well before the era when every vehicle had a trunk release, so every now and then a driver would claim they did not possess the trunk key on their person. The choices for the inspecting agents were to believe the driver and send him north or break open the trunk, with the realization that if that compartment turned out to be empty you had just intentionally damaged that driver's personal property. At that point an agent had to go with his instincts. Did the driver seem calm and unconcerned? Did it appear that there was not a heavy load in the trunk?

I don't remember the make or model, but it was an early 1970s large sedan. The driver, who appeared to be the sole occupant, was a middle age gringo (translation: he was a White guy). He was well dressed and extremely friendly - not your typical smuggler profile. On face value there did not seem to be anything suspicious about the vehicle or driver.

Agent Bill Brown shouted from the point, "Rolodex tail light!"

I do not know if it was a Border Patrol wide phenomenon, but rolodex tail lights were certainly a San Clemente reality. Whenever a vehicle was caught transporting illegal aliens, the details of that vehicle, including make, model, color and license plate number were recorded in a rolodex file that was kept in the station supervisors office. In the pre-computer database age, that rolodex file had very limited applications. There were hundreds of vehicles listed in that file. To check the file to see if a suspicious vehicle had been caught transporting illegals previously, an agent or supervisor would have to flip though many hundreds of cards in the file. There had to be a faster, easier was to identify a vehicle that had been used to smuggle aliens. There was - the rolodex tail light.

There were many procedures to follow involving processing a vehicle that had been used to smuggle illegal aliens. Most of these policies were in writing, but one procedure was never going to be found in a manual. At some point during the process, the apprehending agent would perform a thorough search of the vehicle to inventory its contents. During this inventory search the agent would take a moment to break one of the vehicle's tail lights with his flash light. It certainly was not policy or legal to be damaging private property, but it did provide a quick hint to the agent at the point. When a vehicle was at the stop sign and the point man walked to the rear and noticed the broken rolodex tail light, that vehicle was surely directed to secondary for further inspection.

This sedan now stopped in secondary with its friendly gringo driver had a broken left tail light. Maybe it was just coincidence, and after a quick look in the trunk I would send this affable fellow north. Frank Monte was standing back allowing me to take the lead in this inspection, and my suspicions began to rise when I asked to look in the trunk. The gentleman searched through his key ring and sounded very apologetic in stating that the trunk key was not on the ring. He further stated that the vehicle belonged to his friend, so he did not know where the trunk key was and that he did not even realize there was no trunk key since he had no business requiring him to open the trunk.

This man was not the least bit nervous, and I tended to believe his story, but I could not let this vehicle go without getting a look inside the trunk. Obviously, there was no release for the trunk, but there was another possible method. I explained that I would not break open the trunk, but that I was going to have to go through the back seat. The male remained as cool as a cucumber as he told me to do whatever I believed was necessary. I really wasn't looking forward to this operation. The back seat was bolted in place, so it was going to take a lot of effort to get into that trunk. Before starting the bolt removal process I was able to pull the back seat forward enough to slide my entire arm past it and under the opening to the trunk. I now had another option. I could feel around inside the trunk and if there did not appear to be anything inside I would forgo the seat removal.

I got myself into as comfortable a position as possible and began probing around with my right hand. Almost immediately, something was blocking my hand's progress. There must have been a mop wedged in the back of the trunk that was blocking my hand's path. I grabbed hold of the mop head and pulled and tugged to get it out of the way. It wouldn't budge. I pulled to the right, left, up, and down, but I could not get that mop to move one inch. It must have really been wedged in place somehow.

I came out of the vehicle to catch my breath. I commented to the driver that there was a mop blocking my ability to probe inside the trunk. The male's mood had significantly changed. Smiling and agreeable had turned into nervous and stone faced. "Is there something wrong?" I inquired.

With a look indicative if accepting the inevitable he reached into his pants pocket and produced a single key. "What's the use." he sighed.

The opened trunk revealed four people lying side by side. They were all one family - a middle age husband and wife with their 14-yar old son. Furthest back in the trunk was the wife's 72-year old mother. The mop I had been pulling on with all my might was actually this women's hair. I pulled and tugged for at least five minutes and she never made a sound.

CALL OF THE WILD

Walking the streets of New York City, my vast experience with wildlife included crossing paths with stray dogs, cats, squirrels, and defending myself from the occasional pigeon aerial bombardment.

On face value, the San Clemente checkpoint was not that foreign to what I was accustomed to. The San Diego Freeway was a segment of Interstate 5, a major north–south route of the Interstate Highway System in the state of California. It began at the Mexico-United States border at the San Ysidro crossing and went north across the length of California. This highway links the major California cities of San Diego, Santa Ana, Los Angeles, Stockton, Sacramento, and Redding. Interstate 5 has several named portions. Along with the San Diego Freeway is the Montgomery Freeway, Santa Ana Freeway, Golden State Freeway, and West Side Freeway, The eight lanes of voluminous traffic are a match for any New York City highway.

The work of the Border Patrol agents at the San Clemente station was not confined to the Freeway, as there were alternate routes for illegal aliens that involved circumventing the checkpoint. Although the area west of the highway was used as an alternate path, there really wasn't much area to speak of. The Pacific Ocean loomed about a quarter mile to the west, and between the highway and the ocean were railroad tracks, Old Pacific Coast Highway, and San Onofre State Park and Beach. It was a very limited, narrow path. To the east, however, was the expansive Camp Pendelton Marine Corp base. Camp Pendelton was the preferred route around the checkpoint, so agents from San Clemente spent a significant amount of time beating the bushes in Camp Pendelton. As I would soon learn, however, the Marines and the illegals were not the only living things frequenting the base.

The hour and a half at the checkpoint had made me particularly thirty. Upon relief I strolled into the station and proceeded directly to the soda machine for a refreshing beverage. We were only working with five agents on the shift, so there was no point in going anywhere because I would have to be back out at the checkpoint in less than an hour. I wandered into the administration room while savoring every sip of my soda. Rocky Carter was the station's administrative agent. In years to come I would find that the NYPD would have several names to characterize Rocky's position, such as house mouse, and janitor with a gun.

Rocky Carter was a 50-year old native of Alabama who had been with the Border Patrol for fifteen years. His ample midriff, receding hairline, and ruddy cheeks provided camouflage to a Korean War combat veteran who had won a silver star. Rocky never seemed to get excited or upset, as he meandered through life at one speed - slow. The rumor was that if Rocky was set on fire, he would slowly walk to a hose, take deep breath as he turned on the water, and examine the nozzle a bit before finally dousing the flames. Rocky was a great guy.

As I entered the room, Rocky was seated at the large metal table taking inventory of all the forms used at the station.

"What's up Rock?"

Rocky continued studying the forms through his reading glasses while responding with his usual catchphrase, "Same ol', same ol'."

I walked around the room looking at nothing in particular. I was just killing time while finishing my soda. After a few seconds of silence Rocky looked up from his forms and spoke in his usual slow, measured tone. "Hey Bob. Can I ask you something?"

"Sure Rock. What's up?" Rocky pointed at my belt loops. Speed loaders were not yet a popular method for storing additional ammunition. Border Patrol agents carried their extra ammo in the old style loops on their gun belt. "You don't carry any snake shot, do you?"

"Snake what?"

"Snake shot," Rocky chuckled. "You really are a gangster, aren't you?" To Rocky, everyone from New York City was a ganster. "You do realize that there are some bad boy snakes in them hills don't you?"

"What?" Rocky certainly had my attention.

"When you're lying in the bush working a sensor hit and some bad boy rattler comes up on you, what are you gonna do - strangle it?"

Rocky's point was valid. I had been "laying in the bush" many times, and I had never considered being visited by a rattle snake.

"I don't know Rock. I guess I'd scare him away." I suppose I was equating a poisonous rattle snake to an annoying alley cat I may encounter in New York.

Rocky got up from the table and shook his head as he disappeared in to the locker room. "Gangsters."

A few minutes later Rocky returned and extended his right hand. "Here."

I took the two items from Rocky, but I was not sure what they were. They looked like miniature shot gun shells, but I had never seen them before. Rocky must have sensed my ignorance. "It's snake shot."

"Oh," I said feigning clarity. Rocky sat down at the table and returned to his forms.
"So what do I do with it?"

Rocky looked straight down at the table for a moment, then turned and looked at me above his reading glasses. He had that "you really can't be that stupid, can you?" look on his face. "You load it in your gun. What do you think you do with it. When Mr. Rattler comes a callin out in the boonies - BAM."

I did nothing but continue to exploit my ignorance. "A snake's a pretty small target. What if I miss?"

Rocky was beginning to question how I had managed to survive so far.

"It's snake shot, son. The pellets disperse like a shot gun. It's impossible to miss."

Forty minutes later I was back working secondary at the checkpoint. I had twelve loops on my belt. I removed two .357 magnum rounds and replaced them with the two rounds of snake shot. Come get me Mr. Rattler. I was ready.

It wasn't until I performed a patrol of Camp Pendelton with Agent Floyd Barnes that I really got a feel for what I could run into while working a sensor hit. Floyd Barnes was from Elsa, Texas. I did not know anything about Elsa then, and I still know nothing about Elsa today. I presumed Elsa was a small, rural community because Floyd displayed a knowledge and comfort level with the wildlife in the 125,000 acres of Cam Pendelton that did not seem consistent with two years at San Clemente.

Floyd at first provided an overview of the wildlife situation in the area "Most of these critters want to see you about as much as you want to see them. Still, we're sharing their backyard, so you're bound to run into one or two of them."

I guess I still possessed my predetermined mindset that the world of wildlife consisted of stray dogs and alley cats until I completed that patrol with Floyd Barnes.

Floyd told me that coyotes and snakes were two of the most commonly seen critters here, but he seemed excited in mentioning that if I was lucky, I might also get the rare opportunity to see a bobcat or mountain lion. Mountain lions? This type of luck could pass me by, thank you.

As if mountain lions and coyotes were not bad enough, Floyd transitioned into the wide variety of snakes that called the base home. I was beginning to feel very much like Dorothy in the Wizard of Oz. While Dorothy voiced a very meek and frightened "Oh my" to the warning of Lions and Tigers and Bears, I might just as well have provided my very own wimpy "Oh my" response to Floyd's description of mountain lions, coyotes, and snakes. Floyd continued to say that there were all kinds of snakes on the base, but that I only needed to be worried about the three venomous kinds: the speckled rattlesnake, the red diamond rattlesnake, and the most aggressive and abundant of the three, the south pacific rattlesnake.

How the heck was I supposed to tell a venomous snake from a non-venomous snake? Were they wearing signs? As Floyd continued his lecture I unconsciously fingered the rounds of snake shot in my loops.

"In the spring snakes are all over the place," Barnes related. "Springtime brings them out of hibernation and they start looking for food."

I guess Floyd could sense my apprehension. "Don't worry pardner, unless there is food or water around these critters don't really want any part of us. It's not natural for them."

When we got back to the station, as we walked through the parking lot Floyd hesitated before entering and pointed to the left side of his gun belt. "See this? This is the trophy most of the boys got."

I leaned in closer and squinted. It looked like a small pine cone attached to his belt. "What is it?"

"It's the rattlers from a snake I killed."

I backed up and waved him off. "That's alright Floyd. That's a trophy I can do without."

Illegals who did not choose to risk driving through the checkpoint area had to go around it. As I previously mentioned, they could choose to go west to the beach and state park or they could use Camp Pendelton to the east. Either way, they had to walk around the station. Hence, the term "Walkarounds" was used to describe these illegals seeking to circumvent the checkpoint.

Manpower restrictions did not permit agents to be permanently posted in Camp Pendelton and on the beach, so the main detection weapon to combat walkarounds were sensors. These were the same seismic sensors used by the military in Vietnam. The sensors were buried in shallow ground and had a range in which they would detect movement. The alarm board for the sensors was located in supervisor's office at the station. The key to this sensor detection system lay in the sequence of sensor hits.

The sensors were buried south of the station along the common alien trails about one hundred yards apart. A hit on a sensor meant nothing to the monitoring supervisor because as I had recently discovered, that sensor hit may have been triggered by a mountain lion just as easily as by an illegal. A hit on the next sensor provided cause for concern. If it was a mountain lion, he was walking north along the trail frequented by illegals – not likely. A third sensor hit was the defining moment. This was a group moving north. At that point the supervisor dispatched an agent or agents to respond to the trail where the sensor hit had occurred, and more times than not, within a few minutes the group walked directly into the waiting arms of the agents.

Like anyone else who performs an act repeatedly, illegal aliens learned. Especially the smugglers who guided groups of walkarounds along the trails of Camp Pendelton. After a while the locations of the sensors would become known, so on a regular basis the sensors would be relocated along the trails.

I had just come off the checkpoint for the last time during the shift. As I came out of the men's room my main concern was locating Jim Morgan, the shift supervisor. If he was already out the door, I intended to be right behind him, forgoing any UOT (more on UOT later). That plan was dashed immediately with the sound of Morgan's voice from the supervisors office "Bryan, come here."

Five minutes later I was driving out of the parking lot and up the steep dirt hill to the back road behind the station. My mission was simple. I was to go to one particular trail in Camp Pendelton and relocate the sensors one hundred yards south.

I parked the vehicle at the side of the back road and walked up the steep incline to the walking trail where the sensors were located. I located the sensor without much problem. The top of it was visible but the majority of the sensor was buried in the ground. This sensor had been in the ground for quite a while, and it was not easy getting it out of the ground. I had to return to the patrol car and retrieve a shovel to finish the job. With more manual labor than i really cared to do I finally unearthed the sensor. I carefully carried it down the incline and placed it in the trunk. I had driven about twenty feet before jamming on the brakes and popping the vehicle into reverse. I had forgotten the shovel up on the trail.

A quick climb up the incline brought me back to the trail. But wait - where was the shovel? I quickly realized that I had reversed the vehicle too far. I could now see the shovel lying on the side of the path about forty feet south of me. It was very quiet as I walked. The only sound I could hear was my own steps plodding along the trail. Another sound joined in with my footsteps - a rattling sound. I had never seen or heard a rattlesnake before, but that fact was irrelevant. Bobcats and mountain lions didn't rattle, and unless there was a baby with a rattle hiding in the brush - there was likely a rattlesnake nearby.

I froze in my tracks. My eyes were trying to locate the source of the rattling sound. Suddenly, my eyes stopped scanning. There it was - slithering around about ten feet from me in the dirt area where I had removed the sensor.

Once I had time to reflect, I would have to say that this six foot long multicolored snake was very beautiful, but that was after I was long gone from the area. Rocky had told about the venomous rattlers, but as I stood face to face with this rattling devil I could have cared less whether it was a speckled rattlesnake, a red diamond rattlesnake, or a Brooklyn garden snake. I didn't know what to do.

Back in New York, I had been taught that if I came across a stray dog in an isolated area, the worst thing I could do was run because the dog would chase me. I wondered if the same principle applied to rattlesnakes. If I ran, was this snake going to chase me? That seemed pretty stupid. I never heard of snakes chasing people, but then again what did I know about snakes - nothing!

If I had been in a cartoon, you would have seen the light bulb appear over my head. The snake shot! I never took my eyes from my adversary as I slowly removed my revolver from its holster. I opened the cylinder and removed one round from a chamber. I put the round in my pocket and then went straight to my loops to remove a round of snake shot. I chambered the snake shot and closed the cylinder, making sure the snake shot was at the one o'clock position and would be the next round fired. I took a couple of steps closer and raised my firearm in a combat stance. The rattling was more intense now and the snake raised his head off the ground to face me. This was it - the moment of truth.

The sound was not like a gun shot. It was more like a very loud PUFF, and there was very little recoil. The purpose of the snake shot was to produce a shot gun-like dispersal that would guarantee a hit. As the puff subsided I still heard the rattling - louder and more intense. Worse yet, the snake was still head up and staring at me. Holy shit! Somehow, I had managed to miss - even with the snake shot. Mental note: remember to tell Rocky Carter that it is possible to miss with snake shot.

The snake slowly slithered a few inches in my direction. That was all I needed to see. I would certainly find out now if snakes chased people because I was gone, flying down the incline and into the vehicle. I never even went back for the shovel.

Weeks later I was driving alone down that same back road on my way to meet Marine MPs who had apprehended three illegals. The road was always empty and I was tooling along at a pretty good speed when something caught my eye on the side of the road and brought me to a screeching stop. I got out of the patrol car and walked cautiously, stopping at the rear of the vehicle. About ten yards further back was a long snake laying on the road – a long dead snake that is. What made me stop for this departed reptile were the rattles I observed. This departed fellow was some type of rattlesnake, and here was my golden opportunity to make up for my horrendous snake shot marksmanship and take my rightful trophy.

I found a long stick on the edge of the road and cautiously approached. Even though the snake's head appeared crushed, I still entertained the idea that maybe he was just sleeping, and that I would anger him if I woke him. I moved to within range of my stick and began poking. I was relieved to receive no response. This rattler was deceased. I discarded the stick and replaced it with a knife from my gun belt. I was still very anxious as I cut at the rattlers, and it wasn't until I was safely back in the vehicle with my trophy in hand that I breathed a huge sigh of relief. From that day forward I wore those rattles on my gun belt. Mucho macho. No?

Years later as an NYPD lieutenant, I had to adjudicate a disciplinary case involving a police officer who was wearing commendation breast bars that he hadn't earned. It was enraging to think that this officer was falsely wearing the symbols that were given to officers who had acted bravely and heroically in the line of duty, at great peril to their own safety. At least this officer was painfully honest when confronted with his malfeasance. He simply stated that he wore the unearned commendations because they looked good to girls. This did not excuse his actions, but for some reason, his excuse of wanting to look good transported me back in time to that back road on Camp Pendelton. I was actually no better than this cop wearing phony commendations. I wore those rattles on my belt as a testament to a battle with the deadly snake when in reality I had cut them off a snake who had lost a battle to the tires of a moving vehicle. I wanted to look good and join the club of good ol' boys at the station who wore those rattles as a trophy. Sometimes perspective can be very sobering.

SEARCHLIGHT

It was another beautiful Southern California night. It was around 9:00 PM and I found myself behind the stop sign. The light nature of the traffic presented its own unique problems. When traffic was heavy, the sheer volume forced vehicles approaching the checkpoint to a crawl. Lighter traffic conditions, however, allowed vehicles to maintain highway speed, and the agent behind the stop sign had to rely on the huge flashing signs to prompt vehicles to slow down.

Sometimes, however, huge flashing signs announcing STOP HERE U.S. OFFICERS were not enough. Some people seem to go through life oblivious to what is going on around them, so why would they slow down when approaching huge flashing signs, traffic cones, and a uniformed agent behind a stop sign?

Some drivers may have been consciously blowing through the checkpoint because they were hauling contraband, like drugs or illegal aliens. Other drivers blew through simply because they had their heads up their butts. Regardless of the motivation for the failure to stop, there was a policy to deal with these vehicles that was not found in the Border Patrol Handbook.

A large Maglite flashlight was an essential tool for working the point. At night, it was used to perform a quick inspection of the interior of the vehicle while considering whether to direct it for secondary inspection. The flashlight also served a second essential checkpoint function.

In lighter traffic conditions, the sequence of events for a vehicle approaching the checkpoint at a high rate of speed was usually the same. As the vehicle got within a few hundred feet of the point, I would notice that the vehicle did not appear to be slowing down. As the vehicle drew near, I would supplement the stop sign by waving my hand toward the driver in the universal sign for STOP.

When these visual cues failed, as the vehicle sped past me I would scream at the top of my lungs "STOP!" One final touch to finish off the process involved the Maglite. As I screamed at the passing vehicle, I would also whack the rear of the vehicle with the flashlight, sometimes breaking the tail light. Right or wrong, it was definitely a learning experience for the head up the butt class of driver.

I was about ten minutes into my half hour on the point, and traffic was fairly light. Nothing was going on, and I had not yet directed any approaching vehicles into secondary. Joe Medina and Rich Hunter were working in secondary. Joe was a very distinguished looking tall, lean, 45- year old Mexican-American originally from Nogales, Arizona. He had been with the Border Patrol for eleven years, and I enjoyed working with Joe. While there were some agents at the station who seemed annoyed by my youth and New York City accent (by the way - I still don't think I have any accent), Joe seemed to enjoy the qualities. In fact, we had a NYC based code for use on the radio.

When I first worked at the checkpoint with Joe, he would good naturedly mention that being from New York City, I must know what a *STUNOD* is. I was well aware of the term STUNOD. It derived from Italian, and I believe it meant something like "not paying attention" or "out of tune." In New York City, however, STUNOD was simply Brooklynese for STUPID. I certainly knew the meaning of the term, but to be a smart ass I responded to Joe's inquiry with a straight face, explaining that STUNOD was DONUTS spelled backwards. For some reason, Joe found that response hysterical. If I was patrolling in San Clemente or Oceanside and he was back at the station, he would sometimes come over the radio with the message "STUNOD" in his best attempt at a Brooklyn accent. This was a code to tell me that he wanted me to pick him up some donuts.

Back to the checkpoint. I was busy waving vehicles past on my right and left while Joe and Rich sat comfortably in secondary, waiting for me to direct a vehicle over to them. Out of the corner of my eye I noticed Joe stand and walk a couple of steps in my direction.

"Hey" he yelled from the side of the road, trying to get my attention. I momentarily diverted my attention from the approaching vehicles and looked towards Joe. "Searchlight...10-minutes." Joe retreated to his chair and resumed his position of leisure.

Behind the stop sign, I had no idea what his message was supposed to mean. In retrospect, I suppose I should have turned the stop sign and abandoned the point momentarily to go over to secondary and find out from Joe exactly what this message meant - but I didn't. I remained behind the sign, checking vehicles, quickly forgetting the cryptic message.

Ten minutes later traffic was particularly light, so it was very easy to recognize the approach of one of the aforementioned "head up the butt" types. With its headlights creating glare, all I could tell was that it was a very large sedan, and that it was approaching the point fast. I went through the usual exercise in futility of giving the hand signal for stop with my left hand while my right hand maintained a tight grip on my Maglite. The final act of this drama was complete with my shout of STOP as the vehicle flew past, followed simultaneously with the sound of my Maglite landing on the rear driver's side quarter panel.

As soon as I made solid contact with the flashlight, I instinctively looked at secondary to confirm that Joe and Rich had seen this jerk blow the point. Joe had nearly fallen out of his chair and was now scrambling towards me with a look of astonishment on his face. "What the hell are you doing - Searchlight."

I turned the stop sign and abandoned the point, my arms outstretched in confusion. "What the hell is searchlight?"

"Nixon, Nixon, Nixon." That's the only word Joe kept saying, or at least that was the only word I needed to hear.

It seemed that searchlight was a code no one at the station had managed to tell me about. In his post presidential days, former President Richard Nixon lived in San Clemente. It was fairly common for Nixon to be riding through the checkpoint on his way home. Searchlight was the code used for Nixon. The Secret Service would notify the station with the code to communicate that Nixon would be passing through the checkpoint.

The car had not stopped, but now I was more than a bit nervous. I had just smashed the former President's car with my flashlight. We never said anything about it to the supervisor inside the station, and thankfully, I never heard about the incident from Nixon's end. I guess Joe summed up the incident best standing there with me at the side of the highway. He shook his head and smiled. "You really are STUNOD."

CRAZY

Experts in the field of law enforcement will tell you that policing is overwhelmingly dull, mundane, routine work sprinkled with brief periods of adrenaline pumping excitement and sometimes sheer terror. The Border Patrol checkpoint at San Clemente was no different. There were many times that the checkpoint activities fit nicely into the laid back Southern California style of living. When things were slow at that checkpoint the atmosphere could be so perfect that the danger came from lack of focus. Picture an early evening with the sun setting on the Pacific. A cool ocean breeze feeling so good its making the 80-degree temperature seem therapeutic. Sitting in secondary in these perfect conditions was hypnotic. For all of this time in Shangri-La, however, there were times when the checkpoint went absolutely crazy.

On a rotating basis, agents were assigned to prepare the station's weekly intelligence report. This document was primarily a statistical recap of San Clemente station activity for a particular week. To illustrate the activity occurring at the station, I have included part of an intelligence report I prepared for the period 10/21/79 to 10/27/79.

- A total of 508 apprehensions were made during this period. 503 of this total were deportable aliens.
- A total of 22 smuggling cases involving 25 principals and 117 aliens were apprehended this period.
- Two vehicles involved in smuggling cases were seized. The total estimated value of the vehicles is $6,800.00.
- Three OTMs (Other Than Mexican) were apprehended during this period. Two from El Salvador and One from Peru.

Saturdays and Sundays near the end of the 4x12 shift always had "Crazy" potential. When traffic became too heavy we would shut down the checkpoint and patrol the freeway in marked Border Patrol vehicles. Highway patrol was always good for catching several load vehicles, but in reality, when the checkpoint went down it was like the faucet of illegal aliens was turned up. Their intelligence system was pretty good, so as soon as the checkpoint was down, load vehicles began pouring through north on the freeway.

If I wanted to walk right into some "Crazy" all I had to do was work a midnight shift on a Saturday or Sunday night. When these shifts started, the checkpoint was usually down due to heavy weekend freeway traffic during the 4 x 12 shift. As the midnight shift began, traffic was usually light enough to begin checkpoint operations again. Remember, when the checkpoint would go active the faucet of illegals was still wide open, so once the checkpoint opened the fun began. Load vehicles that suddenly realized the checkpoint was active began bailing out all over the freeway to the south. Other load vehicles tried to run the point resulting in high speed pursuits to the north, and still other loads simply pulled up to the check point an gave up. There were smugglers, illegals, and load vehicles everywhere.

The drivers of load vehicles, who would be criminally prosecuted for alien smuggling, were separated from their loads and placed inside one prisoner processing room. All the illegals from the various loads were put into the large detention cell. It was not uncommon to virtually cease operations an hour into the shift because the station was overflowing with prisoners and every agent working had at least one load and smuggler to process. Finally, when all the bailouts to the south were corralled: the pursuits to the north resolved, and the traffic at the checkpoint apprehended, the checkpoint went down again so that all the prisoners could be sorted out and processed. When operations were suspended it would not be uncommon to have ten drivers (smugglers) and 150 illegals inside the station.

There were some unique methods for keeping control of crazy situations like this. My time at San Clemente was well before the era of the Sharpie marker, but when I first arrived at the station I wondered why there seemed to be an abundance of felt tip Magic Markers. I found out on my first "Crazy" night. Let's say that in rapid succession, three agents brought in three load vehicles. Each vehicle had a driver and ten illegals dispersed throughout the vehicles and their trunks. All these detainees were quickly searched and housed in the station – the three drivers in one holding room and the thirty illegals in the large detention cell. The apprehending agents were then right back to the road for more apprehensions. And so it went.

When the smoked finally cleared and there was a station bursting at the seams with smugglers and illegals, how did we know what smugglers were driving what vehicles and which aliens were in those vehicles? This is where the Magic Markers were indispensable. Immediately after searching a driver, the apprehending agent took a Magic Marker and wrote the license plate number of the vehicle on the driver's forehead. Some may look at this act as not being exactly humane, but it was an effective way of keeping administrative control in these crazy circumstances. As for the illegals, we wrote the license plate number on the back of their hands. When it came time to process we had a means of putting the vehicles, drivers, and loads together.

I don't know what else could have been done to keep control under those circumstances. I'm sure sociologists and experts in police misconduct would point to the act of "marking" people as being dehumanizing, serving as a road map to abuse. I don't know. Maybe they would be right. It was very hard to think of people as individuals when you were running around participating in what amounted to a human version of a cattle round up. Perhaps the activities during these "Crazy" periods provided a conducive environment for darker activities.

TRAIN PATROL

My first experience as a police officer in New York City was as a transit cop, and my first experience as a transit cop was performing train patrol as a member of the tactical patrol force. From 8pm to 4am I rode subway trains all over the city. It took about six months to transfer off train patrol, and as far as I was concerned it was six months too long. I hated train patrol. Rumbling in the subterranean world of NYC during late nights was not my first encounter with train patrol, however. Patrolling the rails was one of my functions while assigned to the San Clemente station.

Illegal aliens who made it across the border and continued north via Interstate 5 had to deal with the San Clemente checkpoint. Actually, they didn't have to deal with the checkpoint. They could attempt to walk around it on the beach or through Camp Pendelton.

 There was still another way to circumvent the check point. Like hundreds of thousands of travelers in this country, they could ride the rails north. Amtrak whizzed right by the checkpoint and was actually the fastest way to get from the border to Los Angeles. To close this loophole, agents from San Clemente would regularly inspect the northbound Amtrak trains.

In looking at a current Amtrak map, there seems to be many more stations going up the west coast then there were in 1980. To my recollection, the next station north of Oceanside was San Juan Capistrano and then Santa Ana. Now, it appears as if there are stations in San Clemente and Irvine. I don't believe these stations existed during my tenure with the Border Patrol.

The train inspection routine called for two agents to drive south to Oceanside. One agent would board the northbound Amtrak train and perform an inspection as the train travelled north to San Juan Capistrano. The other agent would drive to San Juan Capistrano and pick up the agent and any illegal aliens he may have found on the train.

I always found performing these train inspections a little distasteful. I would always think about the movie *The Great Escape*. This 1963 film chronicles the story of a mass escape from a German POW camp during WWII.

Some of the escapees end up on passenger trains and there is a scene where a Gestapo agent walks through the cars demanding "Papers" from those passengers he suspects may be escapees. In essence, I was doing the same thing, walking through the cars, stopping periodically and demanding "Papeles!"

During one particular train inspection assignment on a day shift, I was dropped off at the Oceanside station by agent Robert Lorry. You remember him, don't you? Lorry was the crazy eyed academy classmate who made Steve and I look foolish by giving us camouflage face paint during the night line watch exercise. Yes, this same nut job had been one of four other classmates assigned to the San Clemente station. I exited the Border Patrol van and said, "See you in San Juan."

Lorry's eyes were as crazy as ever as he mumbled, "With the swallows."

What? I guess that was some kind of reference to the swallows returning to Capistrano. Who knows? During the trip north my *Where are your papers* routine netted two illegals. These were two rural boys who may have well as had "undocumented" stamped on their foreheads to complement their straw cowboy hats. They both knew the routine and smiled meekly when I told them to follow me. We were about a minute out of San Juan Capistrano when the train rumbled to a slow stop. The conductor's announcement followed:

" Due to a small fire in the vicinity of the San Juan Capistrano station, this stop will be bypassed. Sorry for the inconvenience. Next stop Santa Ana."

Wonderful. Santa Ana is another 25 miles north of San Juan Capistrano.

I told the boys to have a seat and I joined them in the adjacent row. I may have to wait a while in Santa Ana. Traffic might be heavy going north. A terrible feeling came over me. Lorry would have enough sense to pick me up in Santa Ana, wouldn't he?

When I detrained at Santa Ana I tried to maintain a low profile. This was no easy task. Here was a uniformed Border Patrol Agent walking around with two illegal aliens in tow in an area that wasn't exactly Border Patrol friendly. I don't know how Santa Ana is today, but in

1980 if you woke from a sound sleep near the Amtrak station, you would be hard pressed to determine whether you were in California or Tijuana.

Lorry was nowhere in sight, so I settled down with my two new friends in the most isolated corner of the station I could find. Fifteen minutes later – still no Lorry. At this point, I was beginning to care less and less about my prisoners. I observed a pay phone at the opposite side of the terminal, so I instructed my companions to "wait here" while I walked to the phone.

"San Clemente Border Patrol – Supervisory Agent Munson – May I help you?"

"This is Bryan. I'm in Santa Ana on a train inspection."

"What are you doing in Santa Ana?"

I rolled my eyes. I was tempted to say that I was just doing a little sightseeing. "The train bypassed San Juan, but I don't see Lorry anywhere to pick me up."

Munson directed me to stand by. In the background I could hear Munson on the radio.

"822 – 9116 come in."

Munson was using the radio code for the station (822) and the vehicle Lorry was operating (9116).

"9116 – go with your message 822." Lorry's radio voice was a perfect complement to his eyes – he even sounded crazy.

"What's you location 9116?"

"San Juan Capistrano on a train inspection pick up, but the train appears to be a little late."

Munson's voice reflected the realization that there was only so much you could do to get through to Lorry. "It's not a little late. It bypassed the station. Bryan is waiting in Santa Ana. Just wait there. Don't go anywhere!"

I did not here Lorry respond before Munson was back on the phone with me. "Just take the next southbound to San Juan. It's easier then telling that crazy S.O.B. to drive to Santa Ana. Do you have anyone with you?"

Before I answered I looked over my shoulder toward the other side of the terminal. My two buddies were still seated on the corner bench.

"Yeah, I picked up two on the train. I'll bring them south on the train with me."

The next southbound train was not for thirty-five minutes, so I returned to my discreet seat next to the boys. With more than a half hour to kill my attention turned to a snack bar just outside the station. Again, I gave the direction "Wait here!" Five minutes later I was back with hot dogs, french fries, and sodas for all of us. The boys were ecstatic for their surprise feast. Soon, the train rolled in and we were homeward bound.

When we detrained at San Juan Capistrano, my first observation was Bob Lorry standing next to the Border Patrol van, arms outstretched. As I approached with my buddies, he spoke. "Why didn't you tell me you were going to Santa Ana? I've been waiting here the whole time."

For a millisecond I considered responding to this outrageous statement, but then again, this was Bob Lorry.

MORE RAILS

Who doesn't like trains? Every kid wants a train set and can probably remember the moment of their first ride on that huge commuter train. What is it about trains that makes them such a piece of Americana? Is it their power, the visceral vibrations, or the roar? Is it the strange feeling of stability knowing that the train approaches from the same place, and will always pass on to the same 'vanishing point' in the distance? I don't know, but for whatever the reasons, trains are as American as apple pie and baseball. They are engrained in our culture and folklore. Even some criminal activity, like trespassing on trains possesses a certain romanticism.

Exploring railroads and hopping trains has long had a gritty and romantic luster; trespassing on train tracks embodies adventure. Infamous Depression-era photos depicting train-trespassers hitching rides in search of jobs suggest entrepreneurial doggedness. Even children feel the tug of the railroad's appeal through stories like *The Boxcar Children*, a series of books in which a family of orphaned children intrepidly starts an independent life in an abandoned rail car.

Trespassing on railroad property is a modern-day misdemeanor. Despite the positive cultural associations with train tracks, their danger is far from fictional. In 2013 my son became a conductor with the Long Island Railroad, the largest commuter railroad in the United States. To keep his position, he had to obtain a federal qualification as a conductor from the Federal Railroad Administration (FRA). He brought tons of FRA material home while he was training, including statistics regarding railroad trespassing deaths. I was amazed at how many people in this country die each year while trespassing on railroad property.

In retrospect, I don't know why these statistics illustrating the dangers of the railroad environment impacted me so much. I had experienced the dangers of trespassing on the railroad many years earlier with the Border Patrol.

Besides checking the Amtrak trains, we also had to take a look at the freight trains which provided another means of checkpoint circumvention. On midnight shifts we would drive south to inspect the freights. My memory is a bit hazy here. I have a report that documents a freight train inspection, but I have to give myself a D in report writing because the report documents all activities except the location.

I do not remember any massive freight yards. I believe we would simply travel to a location where the freight trains would lay up temporarily. If I was forced to guess I would say that we inspected the freights in Carlsbad.

One early morning at about 2:30AM I traveled south in a Ram Charger with Joe Medina to inspect the freights. What added additional danger to this activity was that we had no coordination with the railroad police. We were running around those trains not knowing when they may move. When we would turn our flashlights on inside an open boxcar, it was like turning on a light in a dark room and watching the cockroaches scatter. Illegal aliens would be flying everywhere, and the chase was on. A chase that was taking place in dimly lit conditions around active railroad tracks.

These freight trains could be a mile long. If the train was getting ready to move there was not an obvious indicator three quarters of a mile back. At some point during this trackside chase I set my sights on a short chunky guy wearing a cowboy hat. My natural selection instincts were kicking in, directing me towards the weaker prey. Slowly I gained on my target as we ran north, adjacent to the train. I was just about to reach out to grab him, but he must have sensed my close proximity. The cowboy made a sudden move to the left and jumped between cars. He tried to vault over the car couplings as I tried to establish a grip on his shirt collar.

In the distance there were a series of loud bangs in rapid succession. They became increasingly louder until the cars that the cowboy and I were between lurched forward. The engine, three quarters of mile north had made a quick move forward, causing the chain reaction to the rear. Thankfully, the train did not even touch me, and the cowboy was lucky in that the impact knocked him out from between the cars as opposed to under the car. Well, at least I had my prisoner. Joe Medina trotted on the scene, his face red with rage. Joe was a friend who I trusted and enjoyed working with. As a friend, he let me know exactly how he felt about my actions. "Don't you EVER go between cars again. Do you hear me?"

I nodded while hanging my head like a kid being scolded by a parent. Joe was right. In an environment as dangerous as railroad tracks I was just compounding the danger tenfold by going between the cars. I would never make that mistake again.

I wasn't finished making mistakes that early morning. Before I had attempted my roundup of the fleeing cowboy, I had taken two illegals into custody and secured them in the back of the Ram Charger. When I returned to the vehicle with Joe and the cowboy, I had a big surprise waiting. The lock on the back of the vehicle was broken and the Ram Charger was empty. Escaped prisoners were a big deal. I could not begin to imagine the paperwork and discipline I would face. Of more immediate concern, I braced myself for another tongue lashing from Joe. Surprisingly, Joe remained completely calm.

"Hey, don't worry about it. It could happen to anyone."

I still didn't know how to handle the escaped prisoner situation, but Joe quickly fixed the problem by asserting that there were no escaped prisoners. We picked up three more illegals in the vicinity of the tracks giving us a total of four to bring back to San Clemente. Joe coached me through a report where I indicated that there had been damage to the vehicle lock. Nowhere in my report, however, was there any mention of escaped aliens. I would have to remember to get Joe a dozen stunods.

NUDE BEACH

For a Border Patrol Agent, U-O-T were the three most important letters in the alphabet. These letters were the abbreviation for uncontrollable overtime. Once off probation, agents qualified for UOT, which added 25% to their salaries. The program was not a bonus, but was based on the concept that agents would almost always be required to work overtime, so rather than record each hour of OT worked on daily basis, a 25% premium was paid. At San Clemente, UOT translated into the expectation that two extra hours would be worked each day.

There were times when UOT was not advantageous, such as several successive days of spending 4-plus after shift hours processing large loads of illegals. For the most part, however, UOT was a very good thing. If nothing special was happening at the end of a shift, the shift supervisor became the focal point for every agent working. The unwritten rule was that no one went home until the supervisor departed the station. The station parking lot became a caravan led by the shift supervisor because the moment the supervisor was in his car, the line of agents working the shift quickly followed him out the door.

The end of shift tendencies became the most important supervisory habit for an agent to have a read on. A common pre-shift comment might be, "Oh no. I have to get out of here as soon as possible today, but Smith is the supervisor, and he likes to hang around." The bottom line was that if there was nothing special happening, but you had to stay and work your two hours, then you had to find something to do. This usually involved taking a car out and patrolling the surrounding areas.

The day shift had just ended, and the station was extremely quiet. The supervisor had given no indications that he was initiating an exit strategy, so it was clear that I was going to have to find something to do for a couple of hours. My quest for a purpose was quickly solved by Frank Monte who waved a set of car keys in the air and motioned with his head for me to follow him. Two minutes later I was in the passenger seat of a Border Patrol Ram Charger as Frank accelerated north on the Freeway.

Although my main concern was killing two hours I was curious about our destination. "Where are we going?"

"To the beach."

There was an excited tone to Frank's voice akin to a child who was about stray from the boundaries set by his parents.

San Onofre State Beach is a 3,000 acre state park directly west of the San Clemente checkpoint. The beach is 3 miles south of the city of San Clemente on Interstate 5 at Basilone Road. The state park is leased to the state of California by the United States Marine Corps.

Governor Ronald Reagan established San Onofre State Beach in 1971. With over 2.5 million visitors per year, it is one of the five most-visited state parks in California, hosting swimmers, campers, kayakers, birders, fishermen, bicyclists, sunbathers, and surfers. It is named after the fourth-century Saint Onuphrius.

The San Onofre Bluffs portion of San Onofre State Beach features 3.5 miles of sandy beaches with six access trails cut into the bluff above. The campground is along the Old Pacific Highway U.S. Route 101 adjacent to the sand stone bluffs.

Although nudity was prohibited at all parts of San Onofre State Beach, a traditional "clothing optional area" was located at the extreme south end of the San Onofre Bluffs beach, accessed via Trail number 6.

It was another beautiful late afternoon in Southern California. I was beginning to believe that the only weather possible here was "beautiful." Frank exited the freeway at Basilone Road and made a left. The only place for a vehicle to go was to Old Pacific Highway which was the access road to the beach. As we passed the nuclear plant Frank made a statement of his patrol intent.

"Hopefully, we'll see a lot more of that."

He was nodding towards the nuclear plant. I must have had a completely dumbfounded look on my face, resulting in Frank's outburst.

"What's the matter with you? Are you blind?"

Frank brought the Ram Charger to a stop and pointed toward the plant. Specifically, he was pointing at the two huge containment domes.

"Those don't look like anything to you?"

I shrugged in a gesture of confusion. Frank was growing more frustrated.

"Come on. You can't be serious."

I was about to explain that I actually could be serious when I suddenly developed complete awareness. Those two containment domes looked exactly like a pair of giant female breasts. To add to the realism, the two warning lights on top of each dome were of a perfect scale to resemble flashing nipples.

"Oh, I get it."

"Geez, it's about time. Well, we're headed south to the nude beach, so I hope these two babies aren't the only breasts we see today."

From that moment forward, whenever I looked at those containment domes, I was never able to see anything but giant breasts with those blinking nipples as beacons leading a drooling populous towards the nude beach. If you think I'm exaggerating, go online and search for *San Onofre Nuclear Plant Containment Domes* – you'll see.

Frank put the Ram Charger back in drive and we were heading south again. I was certainly happy to be part of Frank's plan, but something wasn't adding up.

"There's no vehicle road at the nude beach, is there?"

"No there isn't," Frank responded. "But this is a Ram Charger. We don't need no stinkin' vehicle road."

We stayed on Old Pacific Highway for about three miles until it ended at a parking lot. The parking lot was near the bluffs that overlooked the beach and the ocean. At the south west corner of the parking lot was a trail that wound through the bluffs and down to the beach. Obviously, this was a walking trail, but that fact was not going to deter Frank. As we slowly eased onto the steep trail I had to voice my trepidation.

"Do you really think this is a good idea, Frank?"

"Don't worry about it."

I had never been on this southern-most portion of the beach and my first impression was how narrow it was. My experience with beaches were exclusively Rockaway and Jones Beaches in New York, both of which had a normal width of over a thousand feet. From my perspective, all these southern California beaches in San Clemente, San Diego, and San Onofre were very narrow. This particular section of beach we had emerged onto was even narrower than the others I had seen. My second impression of the beach was disappointment. This unofficial "nude" section of the beach was virtually empty.

As Frank slowly maneuvered the Ram Charger south on the sand next to the bluffs, the only nudity we observed was a 70-year old man proudly waving in the breeze - and he wasn't waving his arms. When we reached the southern-most section of beach, I couldn't help but jab Frank with some sarcasm. "Well, this worked out really well - thanks."

Frank chuckled. "Bad day, I guess. But we did see some nudity, didn't we?"

"Yeah, some old geezer. Great. Why don't you go check his citizenship."

We both laughed as Frank began turning the Ram Charger north to get back to the access trail.

I mentioned previously how narrow this beach was. This southern-most section of the beach could not have been more than 40-feet wide, so when Frank began making the turn, the Ram Charger had to pass over the soft, wet sand closest to the ocean. BOOM. We both were jarred in our seats.

"What the f......."

Frank was now gunning the engine but we were going nowhere. I jumped out the passenger door and observed the reason for our predicament. The rear wheels of the Ram Charger had sunk into the soft, wet sand. No matter what we tried, there was no way to get the buried wheels free. Although clueless on what to do, Frank was crystal clear regarding what he was not going to do.

"I am not going over the radio to say that we got the Ram Charger stuck on the nude beach."

I couldn't help but state the obvious.

"What do you mean WE got the Ram Charger stuck?"

"Yeah, Yeah. Just stay here with the vehicle."

Frank started walking along the beach toward the access trail.

"Where are you going?"

"To get help, where do you think?"

Thirty minutes went by and I had not seen a soul, not even any nude old men. Then, I began to notice something. Was it my imagination, or did the Pacific Ocean appear to be closer to the Ram Charger than it was a half hour ago. Oh my God, the tide was coming in. Wild thoughts raced in my head. What if Frank had walked back to the station and simply went home, leaving me to explain why one of the Border Patrol Ram Chargers was now floating towards Asia. He couldn't be that unscrupulous, could he? The water was about two feet from the buried tires.

I had just about convinced myself that Frank may very well be that unscrupulous when I observed a sight better than ten beautiful naked ladies on this so-called nude beach. Another Border Patrol Ram Charger had emerged from the trail and was slowly driving towards me. The Ram Charger parked next to the bluffs, as far from the water as possible. Frank emerged from the passenger door.

"What did you do?" I shouted.

As Frank approached me he answered in a lower voice. "I got help. What did you think I did?"

"Couldn't you have gotten help via the radio?

"No way. I walked to the parking lot and called the station from the pay phone."

Just then, I observed the driver emerge from the Ram Charger. It was Joe Medina.

Frank smiled. "I called Joe."

Joe approached with the look of a happy kid on Christmas morning.

"I had to see this for myself. How did you two idiots manage this?"

Self-preservation was urging me to clarify that only one idiot had sunk the vehicle into the sand, but this was not the time. Joe could not stop laughing as he went back to the Ram Charger and retrieved a heavy chain. He tossed the chain to the sand in front of our paralyzed vehicle.

"Put that on." he stated as he re-entered the other Ram Charger.

Joe then carefully made several maneuvers to turn the Ram Charger without coming anywhere near the soft sand. When he finally got his vehicle into the correct position, he leaned his head out the driver's window.

"Attach the chain to the back of my truck."

The Pacific Ocean was beginning to splash against the rear of our vehicle when Joe began to slowly accelerate. Frank was in the driver's seat while I observed from the sand. Ever so slowly the tires began to move until finally, they jumped out of the hole and onto the dry sand. We were mobile again. Joe was still laughing as he retrieved the chain.

"How horny are you guys that you would go through all this just to see some naked women. All I know is that you guys owe me big time."

We followed Joe back up the trail, out of the park and back to the station. Before exiting the Ram Charger, Frank turned toward me.

"See you tomorrow." No other words were necessary.

UNINVITED GUESTS

When I was with the Border Patrol, immigration inspections could be conducted within one hundred miles of the international border. This regulation provided the authority for the San Clemente checkpoint to be operating 66-miles north of the border. The hundred mile rule still exists, but I believe there have been restrictions added. I believe the Border Patrol can only enter private property without a warrant within 25-miles of the border. This rule must have had a tremendous impact on San Clemente's farm and ranch operations. Most of San Clemente's operational area was more than 25-miles from the border, so no longer could agents just swoop in from all directions into the farms and ranches because it was all private property.

City patrol was still fair game within the one hundred mile limit. The reality for agents at the San Clemente station was that any enforcement activity that was not on the highway, beach, in Camp Pendelton, on farms & ranches, or involved a train or bus, was city patrol.

City patrol was a great activity for UOT. When the regular shift was over and the oncoming shift had taken over the checkpoint, the easiest way to pass the two hours of UOT (if it actually had to be worked) was to grab a vehicle with another agent and go out on city patrol. More times than not, city patrol was actually an excuse to visit a certain store or restaurant, but it passed the time.

"Let's go!" Joe Barton waved a set of keys at me as he exited to the station parking lot. It had just become apparent that our shift supervisor on the day tour was hanging around, so I was going to have to find something to do for my UOT. Joe Barton was the answer.

Joe drove the Border Patrol van south on the freeway. According to Joe, our destination was the community of Encinitas. Joe had not chosen Encinitas because of some intelligence regarding illegal aliens. There was a certain auto parts store he needed to visit on Santa Fe Drive because it had a part for his truck that he could not find anywhere else. I was absolutely fine with the reason for our trip south on UOT.

I liked Joe Barton a lot. He was 35-years old and had been with the Border Patrol for 10-years. He had been assigned to San Clemente for four years, having previously worked at the Sierra Blanca station, wherever the heck that was. Joe was extremely sociable, knowledgeable, and helpful. The only negative with Joe was his hair trigger temper. I witnessed his explosions of temper several times, not just with aliens, but also with other agents who may have said the wrong thing at the wrong time.

Encinitas was primarily a very nice beach community approximately 25-miles south of the San Clemente checkpoint. There was a "Sketchy" area of town east of the beach area. Joe's auto parts store was in a strip mall on Santa Fe Drive at Gardena Road – right in the middle of "Sketchyville."

I remained in the van while Joe was in and out of the store in under two minutes. "The part's not in yet. I'll have to come back tomorrow."

Oh well, Joe may have been disappointed, but from my perspective the trip was still worthwhile by chewing up the UOT time.

Santa Fe Drive led directly to the freeway entrance. At the intersection of Santa Fe Drive and Gardena Road we stopped for a red light. On the southeast corner of the intersection I noticed a single person. It was a short, thin Mexican male with a baby face who looked to be about 18-years old. The kid was wearing a white "Wife Beater" tee-shirt and was heavily tattooed on both arms. He looked like the stereotypical East L.A. "Cholo."

I wasn't the only one who noticed this kid because when he saluted our Border Patrol van with his middle finger there was an instant eruption from Joe. "Fuck me? Now it's gonna be fuck you!"

Joe stepped hard on the gas pedal and the van screeched as it made a hard left turn toward the cholo. Instantly, the kid was gone, running like the wind south on Gardena Road.

I just assumed the incident was over, and that Joe would turn back onto Santa Fe Drive and continue to the freeway. I was wrong! Joe continued to gun the engine as we raced south down Gardena Road, with the youth still in sight as he continued his sprint.

We were speeding down a residential block of single story ranch homes – all of them looking exactly the same. There were two big differences I found in the residential communities in Southern California as opposed to New York City neighborhoods. In Southern California, everything seemed to be one level and more spread out. If a giant hand came down on a residential New York City neighborhood and squashed it down, you would end up with a Southern California neighborhood – all one level and more spread out.

The kid was now more than two blocks from Santa Fe Drive and I was beginning to see something that I did not like. About a half block further south were people – lots of people. There was a fiesta taking place and there had to be a hundred people gathered around one of the identical ranch homes. Mexican music blared and many of the party goers appeared to have been drinking for many hours.

The kid ran right into the midst of this jamboree, and I just assumed our chase had to be over now. I was wrong again. Without a word of warning the van was parked and Joe was out and wading through the drunken throng, trying to get at the kid.

What was I going to do now? I could not just sit in the van with the windows rolled up and the doors locked. As crazy as this was, I had to help my partner.

I tried to ignore all the cursing and shouting directed at me as I followed Joe's path into the back yard. The kid had apparently entered the home through the back door and Joe was trying to break the door down with his shoulder. This was unbelievable. In about two minutes we were both going to be strung up as piñatas.

Before I could even begin to envision how I would look hanging from a tree being beaten with stick, a more immediate concern arose.

"Pinche Migra!"

The less than hospitable greeting was coming from about 25-feet to my left. A short, fat, middle age Mexican male was slowly staggering towards me.

More concerning than this drunken lout was what the lout was carrying. He needed both hands to support the very heavy, thick tree limb. The man looked much like a drunken baseball player ready to swing, except that I seemed to be the baseball.

Joe Barton became the last thing on my mind. I turned towards the drunk, drew my 357 magnum and aligned my sights as I had been taught in the academy. The look in my eyes along with the barrel of the gun pointed directly at his chest must have penetrated his drunken stupor. The tree limb was down and the drunk was staggering back towards the front of the house. Aside from my inaccurate shot at the snake, this was the closest I came to discharging my firearm with the Border Patrol.

I holstered my revolver and turned my attention back to Joe Barton. Thankfully, Joe had lapsed into a lucid moment because he grabbed me by the arm and began pulling me towards the front of the house. "Let's get the fuck out of here!"

The hoots and hollers were punctuated by a few bottles breaking nearby, but thankfully, none of them found their intended targets. We made it back to the van and within five minutes we were homeward bound on the freeway.

No words were exchanged during the drive north, but as we got within a few miles of the checkpoint I figured I had to say something. "That was interesting. Is that how you usually conduct a city patrol?" Joe did not respond, but he did smile.

TONK

For me, I can trace the entire mess to nothing more than routine duties and some words. The probation, C&E and ten month exam ordeal was in the rear view mirror. I had settled into Border Patrol life at the checkpoint. I had just caught a vehicle at the checkpoint carrying three illegals in its trunk, and I was now sitting at the typewriter in one of the station's prisoner processing rooms, typing up my "catch."

The San Clemente station was "L" shaped with the main entrance being at the point where the two arms of the L met. One arm of the L contained the administrative offices and locker rooms while the other arm was for prisoner processing. A walk down the prisoner processing hall revealed four small prisoner processing rooms, each equipped with two tables and typewriters. At the end of the hall was the heavy security door of a large holding cell. This cell had wooden benches lining its perimeter and could hold about fifty prisoners comfortably, and a lot more uncomfortably.

My three trunk occupants were standing in front of my table in single file. I loaded a fresh I-213 into the typewriter and began working on the male standing first in line. The three men standing before me would only take a few minutes to process. The I-213 was the form used to "VR" or voluntarily return an illegal alien to Mexico. A VR was not considered a criminal arrest, and once this one page form was completed, the alien was placed on an immigration bus that came through San Clemente every few hours and transported south to the San Ysidro port of entry. Once off the bus the aliens were directed into Mexico via a turnstile that you might see used in a subway system. It was as simple as that.

It is also ironic to note that the I-213 was routinely referred to as a "Lie – 213" by the agents because there was no meaningful verification of the information being provided. The male I had locked in the holding cell at the end of the hall would take much longer to process. He was the coyote, and he was being criminally prosecuted for alien smuggling. In reality, he was probably just a poor wetback who the real coyote had ordered to drive when they entered the load vehicle near San Ysidro. San Clemente

Border Patrol policy was quite simple – "You're the driver, then you're the smuggler."

Voluntary Returns were only available to Mexicans. OTMs (other than Mexican) were not simply herded through the Tijuana turnstiles. OTMs were the subject of formal deportation proceedings to their countries of citizenship.

This policy resulted in two types of "false claims" for agents to investigate. Obviously, there were numerous false claims of US citizenship, but due to the VR policy of dropping Mexicans off at the border with Tijuana, there was great motivation for OTMs from South America to falsely claim Mexican citizenship. A Border Patrol Agent who was able to "Break" a false claim by getting the alien to admit that he was not an American or Mexican citizen, was routinely praised by station supervision for displaying outstanding investigative abilities. Stay tuned - more on breaking false claims to come.

As I completed my Lie-213 for trunk rider #1, Jake Sheldon entered the room with an alien he had just pulled off a Greyhound bus. All northbound buses on the freeway were required to stop near the station's front entrance so that an available agent could board the bus and perform an immigration inspection.

Next to my 23-years of age, Jake was the youngest at the station at 24. Jake was from somewhere in North Dakota, and had been with the Border Patrol for a little over two years. He was short and thin – almost frail looking, and during our few conversations he expressed a desire to transfer to the northern border, preferably in North Dakota. My very unprofessional analysis of Jake indicated that he suffered from a severe Napoleonic Complex. Maybe it had to do with his short stature and slight build, but it was my impression that he was constantly concerned with not being "disrespected" by any of the aliens.

Jake was beginning to work on his own Lie-213 as I began interviewing my second customer. My first alien was from Jalisco, and when #2 also indicated he was from the same state, I inquired as to whether they knew each other and were together. #2's response was "Si-mon."

Jake sprung from his chair like he had been shot out of a cannon. He went right for my current interview subject, grabbing him tightly with both hands by his collar and pulling the frightened man's face to within a few inches of his growling mouth "No si-mon, cabron."

"Si Senor, Si Senor" The look of fear on the man's face was palpable.

Jake released his grip and returned to his typing. As he pecked at the keys with two fingers he provided commentary to his action. "Don't take no shit from these tonks."

I had stopped typing. I didn't understand Jake's sudden lunge for my subject and I understood even less what "shit" I had taken. "What are you talking about?"

"Si-mon, man. Don't let him insult you with that cholo si-mon shit."

"What?" I was confused. I had only recently gotten off probation, but I had heard "si-mon" used repeatedly, and I did not associate the term with the disrespectful meaning that had prompted Jake's reaction.

One of the factors that I was beginning to understand, and which I would gain greater insight into as I gained experience was that Spanish has a lot of similarities to English. There are many subtleties to the languages in which meanings can change to the same words based on the inflection or tone. Additionally, there are geographical differences to consider. There are many differences in the meanings of words used in Mexican Spanish as opposed to Puerto Rican Spanish. Furthermore, there are differences in the Spanish used in northern Mexico versus the southern part of the country. The best way I can illustrate the subtleties in words is to cite the movie *Donnie Brasco*. The star of the movie is attempting to explain what the term *"forget about it"* means when used by a NYC mafia gangster, and he comes up with five different meanings based on the context of its use.

Some people, like Jake, were firm in their belief that "simon" was a disrespectful way of addressing someone that was commonly used by "cholos" in the gang culture of East Los Angeles. There was another camp, however, that insisted the word was benign – nothing more than a slang way of saying "yeah, yes, or of course."

There were two other statements made by Jake that puzzled me. First, was his warning to not accept the use of "si-mon" because it was "Cholo shit." Even with my limited experience I was familiar with the term "Cholo."

A cholo was a term used for a Hispanic male that typically dressed in chinos, a wife beater sleeveless tee shirt or a flannel shirt with only the top buttoned, a hairnet, or with a bandana around the forehead, usually halfway down over the eyes. Cholos often had black ink tattoos, commonly involving Catholic imagery, or calligraphy messages or family names. Cholos were a common sight buzzing down the freeway in their low-riders. What I found so perplexing about Jake's outburst was that the old boy he had yanked by his collar and his buddies were from the hill country of Jalisco – about as far removed from being a "Cholo" as possible.

There was another word Jake used that was foreign to me. He had warned me not to take any shit from these

"Tonks." I had heard the term used repeatedly at the station, so obviously it had something to do with illegals. In fact, there were many slang words used for illegal aliens, such as wetbacks, wets, mojados, and pollos. I was familiar with all these terms but I had never asked the origin of tonk.

The next day I found myself working the checkpoint in secondary with Jake Sheldon. As we both leaned on the side of the pursuit vehicle, I recalled my question from the prior day. "Hey Jake, what's a tonk?"

"It's a wetback, man!"

"I could figure that much out." I responded with a touch of annoyance. "Where does the word come from?

"Oh, It's the sound a wet's head makes when we smash it with a flashlight."

I stared at Jake with my head slightly tilted like a confused puppy.

Jake provided clarification by pulling his Maglite from its holder and taking a wild swing at a phantom head.

"TONK." He shouted at the imaginary moment of impact. "Get it now?" he asked through playful laughter.

Jake Sheldon's demand for respect was not a unique attitude at the San Clemente Station. In some respects, it was a very necessary attitude. One might argue that there are many law enforcement agencies that make highway car stops, and that these agencies do not maintain a militaristic discipline over their detainees. I would argue that the highway patrols throughout the country do not have to sit alone in the weeds in total darkness, tasked with the responsibility to surprise, apprehend and control twenty illegal aliens who had just activated a seismic sensor on some isolated back road. The ability to show strength and take control was critical for an agent's safety. The problem was the extremely fine line between an authoritative command presence and abuse. Quite possibly, it was words – words like "Tonk" that were the swords that began punching holes in that line, creating the cavity that eventually pulled several agents to the dark side and left me holding onto the line for dear life.

SHORTCUTS

In November 1989 I bought my first, and to date, only house. I instantly hoped to transform myself from a person with hopelessly little knowledge and aptitude regarding home renovations and repairs, into Queens, New York's version of Bob Villa and This Old House. I read books and purchased tools in an attempt to enhance my skills and ultimately save money.

My first big project (big for me, at least) was to build and install a space-saving folding table in my kitchen. The table was attached to the kitchen wall, but took up very little space because the largest portion of the table was a leaf on hinges that hung down vertically. The leaf was raised and braced only when the table was being used. I followed all the instructions in my book in cutting the wood to size, and sanding and finishing each piece. I attached the hinges as directed by the book, leaving the attachment to the wall as the only remaining task.

The directions for attaching the table to the wall required the use of specific screws and hardware to anchor the table safely to the wall. I was in a hurry to finish my project and thought I knew better at this point. I did not have the specific hardware the directions were calling for, but I had similar hardware. Frankly, it was too much effort to drop everything to run out and shop for the correct hardware when the hardware I had would do the job just as well. I finished the installation with my hardware, and the table was a beautiful sight to behold.

I was a sergeant at that time, and when I was working 4 x 12 tours, how nice it was to be able to sit with my wife in the mornings and enjoy a leisurely breakfast in my self-created breakfast nook. The beautiful breakfasts ended right in the middle of some scrambled eggs one morning about six months after the installation. The entire table, along with the coffee, orange juice, plates, utensils, and food, went crashing to the floor right between my wife and me. I was shocked. How could this have happened to my precious table? The answer should have been obvious. Instead of following the directions regarding the anchorage and doing it right, I had taken a shortcut because it was easier and I believed it would still work. I was wrong, and it was particularly infuriating to me because it was a lesson

I should have learned years earlier at San Clemente. Shortcuts have a way of coming back to bite you.

Border Patrol work was all patrol and field work. At San Clemente, that meant working the checkpoint, patrolling the freeway, working Camp Pendelton and the beach, and raiding the local farms and ranches. Investigations were generally not part of the job description. The Immigration & Naturalization Service had criminal investigators, and the Border Patrol had agents detailed to the Anti-Smuggling Unit (ASU). The closest thing agents at the station encountered that required anything close to an investigation were "False Claims."

As I mentioned in an earlier chapter, false claims came in two varieties – falsely claiming US citizenship and falsely claiming Mexican citizenship to avoid formal deportation proceedings to a South American country. The investigation, or skill involved with false claims was being able to "Break" the claim through interrogation and get the subject to admit their lie. Some false claims were ridiculously easy to break.

Typical in this category would be Manuel. Manuel lives in a ranchita of 600 people in a valley in Southern Mexico. He is 38-years old and has lived in his small village his whole life. As a matter of fact, up until now he has never traveled beyond a fifty mile radius from his small town. Like most of his neighbors, Manuel is a "campesino" who works in the fields. He has a wife and two children, with another on the way, and like any man living under these conditions, he is looking for a better life for his family. Over the years Manuel has heard the stories from neighbors of the money to be made by traveling north to America. One day, he finally decides to try the path north to see if he can make some money and then return home. Manuel speaks no English and knows nothing about America or its institutions. He certainly has not had the forethought to create some backstory to fool La Migra if he is apprehended. Manuel has simply been instructed by a coyote say "U.S. Citizen" if apprehended by the Border Patrol. It would take less than thirty seconds to break this type of false claim.

On the other end of the false claim spectrum is Jose. Jose is also 38 years old and lives in Mexico City. Jose graduated high school and speaks some English. He has access to television so he is able to keep up with world events and American institutions. Jose is single, and has been working various factory jobs on a sporadic basis over the years. His goal for the past five years has been to make it into America and start a new life. To obtain his goal, he has been saving money and preparing. He has paid a smuggler to provide him with false documents as well as assistance crossing the border. The smuggler has told Jose that with his English ability and urban look, his best course of action would be to claim US Citizenship if apprehended by La Migra. To support his claim, Jose is provided with a birth certificate from Elmhurst General Hospital in New York City. He also has the address of the apartment in the Corona section of Queens, NYC where he supposedly spent the first seven years of his life. He even remembers that Ms. Wells was his first grade teacher at PS 133 in Queens. His backstory is that his parents entered America illegally and traveled to New York City, where his father had a cousin who worked for a landscaper. Jose was born in New York City and spent his first seven years there. When his father died in a bar fight, Jose's mother packed up and took Jose back to Mexico. Jose is even able to produce from his pocket his most prized possession - two ticket stubs from a Mets game he attended at Shea Stadium with his father a week before he died. If Jose sticks to his story, he will be extremely tough to break. Remember, on the side of the San Diego Freeway or sitting at a desk at the San Clemente Border Patrol station, no one is calling the Department of Health in New York City to verify the authenticity of the birth certificate. No one is searching through a Queens, New York phone book to see if they can call anyone at the address Jose provided to see if any neighbors ever heard of him. No one is calling the Immigration Office of Criminal Investigations in New York City to ask them to immediately go out into the field and verify the story of one false claim being detained at San Clemente. If Jose hangs tough with his story, it will take much skill in interrogation techniques to make him admit his lie.

Let's pause for moment and think about this. Maybe there is another way to break Jose without hours or days of investigation and interrogation. Maybe there is a shortcut. Suppose we just bounce Jose off the walls a few times or make him hold a chair straight out in front of him and give him a few friendly raps to the back of his head every time the chair begins to lower. That should do the trick, right? I know it would work on me. I would admit to being a citizen of mars if it meant I could put that chair down or stop being the human pin ball in the room.

Let's start connecting the dots. Start with an atmosphere where the environment of routinely being vastly outnumbered by the illegals in remote, isolated locations results by necessity in an agent developing an authoritative command presence when dealing with detainees. This is a good thing. This is a positive instinct for survival. But now factor in the all too common over the top demeanor of the Jake Sheldon's at the station and it is no longer a positive situation. In fact, it was a recipe for disaster. The first ingredient in the recipe was the legitimate motivation of many agents to establish their reputations as experts in breaking false claims.

There were some agents who were outstanding at maintaining a dialogue with a false claim until the detainee would finally slip up in his story and be forced to come clean. Add to the pot a healthy helping of agents desperately seeking that expert reputation, but who had not developed the skills to make the reputation a reality. These, agents, however, were willing to take the shortcuts and get physical to break a claim. Finally, add a pinch of agents who simply enjoyed being heavy handed. Mix it all up and what did you get. You got the Office of Professional Responsibility in Washington DC opening an investigation into numerous claims of abuse and civil rights violations by agents at the San Clemente station.

DEADLY PURSUITS

While at the academy I wondered why such an emphasis was placed on driver training, and in particular on high speed pursuits. The San Clemente checkpoint provided the answer. High speed pursuits were a fact of life that sometimes produced tragic consequences.

The local newspapers would regularly run stories highlighting the danger of Border Patrol high speed pursuits. Vehicle chases by US Border Patrol agents had ended in several deaths and numerous injuries during the span of a decade. The stories would also emphasize the financial cost of these chases. Area hospitals and taxpayers were stuck with hundreds of thousands of dollars in unpaid medical bills for injured immigrants and bystanders. The bottom line in all these stories was that the deadly pursuits almost always started over immigrant smuggling - a crime that the court system treated as minor. Smugglers in cases involving high-speed chases often spent less than two years in prison and charges were rarely brought against the immigrants riding as passengers. A male who lost his wife as the result of a high speed chase was quoted, "How can the Border Patrol be so callous?"

The image the media was portraying of the Border Patrol high speed pursuits at the time reminded me of a line in a movie I saw some years later. In Crimson Tide, Gene Hackman is the captain of a nuclear submarine. At one point, in justifying his actions to his executive officer, Hackman states, "What'd you think, son? That I was just some crazy old coot, putting everyone in harm's way as I yelled "YEE-HA!"

I believe that was how the media viewed the Border Patrol. That we barreled down the freeway putting the life and limb of everyone in our path in jeopardy while we yelled "YEE-HA!" You know something. I don't know if the media was that far off base.

I was never a big fan of these high speed pursuits. I always tried to look at the situation as risk vs. reward. Was it worth the risk to everyone around us to catch a few illegals, and was it devastating if a chase got called off and a few more illegals joined the millions already in this country. On the other hand, I could understand the philosophy of most of the veterans at the San Clemente station. If the smugglers knew that all they had to do to get away from the Border Patrol was to drive away at a high rate of speed, then every smuggler driving north would be tooling down the freeway at 100 mph. Hmm, I guess they had a point too.

What I did not like was the unofficial peer pressure exerted regarding high speed pursuits. There was definitely an underlying "macho" tone that looked down upon an agent who called off a pursuit because the conditions were too dangerous.

Before that morning in May of 1980, I had been involved in several high speed pursuits on the San Diego Freeway. The first pursuit that ended in an incident occurred while I was still on probation.

It was very close to the end of a 4 x 12 shift and the checkpoint was down. I was sitting on an incline on the side of the freeway in the driver's seat of vehicle 9108. Agent John Aponte was with me as we both watched the passing northbound freeway traffic. I was about five minutes away from rolling down the incline and returning to the station parking lot when there was a crackle on the radio.

Frank Monte had started his midnight shift a little early so that he could go north to San Clemente. His intent was not to get an early jump on some city patrol. To the contrary, Frank was tasked with the responsibility of bringing back Kentucky Fried Chicken for the entire oncoming midnight shift. Sometimes, however, reality gets in the way of the best laid plans. Franks voice followed the radio crackle.

"822 – 9130. I'm following a blue, Chevy van northbound on the freeway. The van looks loaded and is refusing to stop."

I rolled off the incline, but instead of drifting back to the station I was accelerating north on the freeway. John Aponte expressed our intentions over the radio.

"9108 will back up 9130."

I made visual contact with 9130 as we crossed into San Juan Capistrano. I fell in behind 9130 as the van exited on the Ortega Highway off ramp. The van turned west on Ortega Highway and continued through three red traffic signals. The van then slowed to approximately 5-10 miles per hour and started riding along the right curbside lane. I was third in line behind the van and 9130, and with a large intersection approaching I saw an opportunity.

I swung out to the left and accelerated past 9130 and the van. I then cut in front of the van, placing 9108 at a 45-degree angle to the approaching vehicle. The van was now boxed in with no place to go. John and I were quickly out of 9108, ready to pounce on the van driver. But wait a minute – the van was still moving. Worse yet, there was no one in the driver's seat of the van. All I could make out was a streaking figure disappearing into the wooded area on the south side of Ortega Highway. Next, was the sound of metal meeting metal as the front of the driverless van smashed into the right rear quarter panel of 9108.

Inside the van, twelve shaken, but uninjured illegal aliens lay all over the rear compartment. The driver of the van was gone into the night. In this incident I experienced a similarity between the Border Patrol and the NYPD. The NYPD is renown for voluminous paperwork, especially for a department vehicle accident. I found the same to be true for the Border Patrol. I spent more time writing up the details of the accident involving 9108 than Frank Monte spent processing the van and twelve illegals inside.

I never liked these vehicle pursuits because of what could happen, and in the May 1980 case, what did happen.

There was a monthly shift rotation at the San Clemente station. Agents worked a month on the 8:00 AM to 4:00 PM tour; a month of 4:00 PM to 12:00 AM; and finally a month of 12:00 AM to 8:00 AM.

This particular weekday midnight tour had been completely unremarkable, and was just about over. Right around shift change there always can be a bit of confusion. Sometimes one of the agents at the checkpoint needed to go into the office a little early, so the relief from the incoming shift had to come out to the checkpoint a little earlier. Sometimes, as was the case on this morning, the agent who was with me in secondary retreated to the office before his relief from the day shift had come out of the office. It was really no big deal to be alone in secondary – except if something happened. In this case, "something" was three separate vehicles approaching the checkpoint and screaming to the primary agent that a vehicle that had just passed the checkpoint had rammed their vehicles as it weaved all over the road.

My good friend Rick Sanders was working the day shift. He was not scheduled to be in secondary, but when I jumped in the pursuit vehicle and radioed the situation, Rick ran out of the station as I passed by and jumped in the passenger seat.

As I picked up speed northbound on the freeway, we received more information via the radio. We were looking for a dark station wagon with Florida license plates. From Oceanside up to our checkpoint, the station wagon had either sideswiped or rammed three different vehicles as it traveled recklessly up the freeway.

Rick had activated our vehicle's amber light as I accelerated north in the left lane, both of us scanning the traffic ahead. Almost in unison, we both blurted "There he is!"

It was a dark colored 1975 Mercury Montego station wagon with Florida plates. The station wagon was in the center lane traveling at approximately 60 mph when I nestled in directly behind it as Rick activated our lights and siren.

We were approaching El Camino Real, the first exit in San Clemente. The station wagon very deliberately exited via the off ramp and continued onto El Camino Real, which is the main drag through the city of San Clemente. He was not speeding or weaving at this point, but he also was not stopping. About a quarter mile into our ride along El Camino Real, the station wagon turned right into a gas station. It did not pull up to the gas pumps, but instead pulled to the rear of the station. I pulled to a stop about twenty-feet behind the station wagon. From our perspective, Rick and I could only see the driver of the vehicle. There were no other visible occupants and the driver appeared to be a White male with long hair.

Rick utilized the PA system in our vehicle.

"Driver, exit the vehicle with your hands up."

There was no response so Rick repeated the order. Still no movement. Rick started to open the passenger door while stating, "I'm gonna approach."

I began to open the driver's door. My intention was to follow my car stop training by using the driver's door as cover as Rick approached the station wagon. I got one foot out of the vehicle and Rick was no further than the front hood when the tires on the station wagon screeched as it sped out of the gas station and turned north on El Camino Real.

The station wagon led us on a ten mile traffic laden, high speed chase on El Camino Real, the Pacific Coast Highway, and Del Obispo Street. During the pursuit we were joined by the San Clemente Police Department and the California Highway Patrol. At one point on PCH the station wagon slowed, and the driver appeared to be furiously reaching for something in the back seat. Rick read my mind. "Oh boy, this lunatic is looking for his gun."

The station wagon picked up speed again and was traveling at a very dangerous 50 mph as it entered San Juan Capistrano on Del Obispo Street. It was just before 8:00 AM on a Thursday morning – the middle of the morning rush hour. The station wagon maintained its high rate of speed as it approached the intersection with Camino Capistrano. The traffic signal was red for vehicles traveling on Del Obispo as the heavy volume of east and westbound traffic glided through the intersection. I was on the brake as I looked ahead in horror. There were no brake lights illuminating on the station wagon and there was no way he was going to be able to snake through the wall of traffic at the intersection.

"Oh my God, he's not slowing down." I yelled to Rick, sensing the inevitable.

From my perspective it was like a bomb had exploded directly in front of us. The station wagon was still traveling at least 50 mph when it t-boned an eastbound late model gold Ford LTD. The severity of the impact drove the LTD 115 feet to the north before settling to a stop on the sidewalk. Both vehicles were virtually destroyed, but there was no time to assess any damage. With the fresh memory of the driver furiously reaching into his back seat, Rick and I were on him in an instant, dragging him out of his shattered vehicle. We found no gun, but what we did discover were some very bizarre circumstances.

The driver was a 38-year old German citizen. His documents of German citizenship as well as his passport were in order. His passport reflected that he had made numerous trips to Venezuela in 1975. The station wagon was legally registered to him in Florida, and it contained a lot of French currency strewn all over the interior of the vehicle. He also had in his possession blank checks from a Venezuelan bank, and a letter written in French with an Armenian letterhead. A subsequent blood test revealed no drugs in his system, but there was something very wrong with this guy.

He wasn't visibly injured in the crash, so I securely held onto our rear-cuffed prisoner while Rick searched the car. He spoke perfect English, and the entire time I held him he was rambling, saying things like he was the president of the United States and why didn't we have a sense of humor. Every time I would turn my head away, he would state, "Turn around, I want to look in your eyes." It was eerie.

While this mope came out of the crash virtually unscathed, the same could not be said for his victim. The 46 year old resident of Dana Point was the owner of a construction company and was going to work like he did every morning, to earn a living to support his wife and three daughters. Everyone at the scene tried their best administering CPR. The efforts were to no avail, however, as the victim was pronounced dead on arrival at San Clemente General Hospital due to a ruptured aorta. The next day the following article appeared in a local newspaper

DEATH RIDES HIGHWAY ONCE AGAIN

A car is involved in two hit-and-run crashes. The driver flees. Police officers pursue. And a man dies. Not the fleeing suspect. Not an officer. But an innocent motorist, cut down yesterday morning in San Juan Capistrano only because he "happened to be there at the time." This is not the first time a high speed pursuit of a suspect has ended in a smash-up in this area. And, judging from the results of our last pleas to find an alternative to this madness, it will certainly happen again. There but for the grace of God go all of us who venture onto the highway. Who can say how many other South County motorists faced death in connection with this chase as it weaved its destructive way from Oceanside, through San Clemente, Capistrano Beach and into San Juan Capistrano where it ended in tragedy. The sad truth is that all of us are potential innocent victims as long as people keep committing crimes and police officers keep chasing them at unsafe speeds.

All these years later and this incident and this article still bothers me. I believed I was doing the right thing. This wasn't a case of allowing a few more illegals to get through. This was an out of control vehicle that had already hit three vehicles as it sped recklessly up the highway. I know I wasn't driving down the road yelling "YEE HA" as I pursued this guy. I pursued him because I believed he presented an immediate danger to those around him. Who knows? Maybe if I hadn't chased him no one else would have been hurt that morning. One thing I can say for sure is that if I had not chased him, that poor man whose only crime was being in the wrong place at the wrong time as he drove to work, would not have been killed on that day. And that fact still haunts me.

PARANOIA

Paranoia: a tendency on the part of an individual or group toward excessive or irrational suspiciousness and distrustfulness of others.
Webster's Dictionary

The rumors and leaks were likely by design. The Office of Professional Responsibility had sent undercover agents posing as illegals into San Clemente. It didn't take much for a rumor of this nature to begin spreading like wildfire among the agents. On face value, such a rumor should not have caused much of a stir. What did it matter if OPR sent a hundred undercovers through the illegal alien apprehension and detention process? Why did the prospect of undercover agents in our midst create such fear? The answer was quite simple.

Considering the entire border patrol agent population at San Clemente, the number of heavy-handed agents was minimal – but there were enough to be problematic. If the investigation was potentially going to touch only those agents who had gone overboard in their handling of the illegals, I don't think the climate of paranoia would have developed. Just as it is challenging to prevent the spread of cancer in the body, it is similarly challenging to keep the scope of an investigation of this nature from spreading. Although there were very few agents who may have actually used excessive force against an undercover agent, the real possibility existed that numerous agents may have been present when the force was used. This was just the reality of the physical layout of the San Clemente Station. Two agents were usually processing illegals in one room, and other agents were constantly walking up and down the halls of the detention processing area. The chances of multiple agents witnessing an act of overzealousness were enormous. It was with this reality that the paranoia spread. Not so much by the very small numbers of force users, but by the much larger numbers of agents who may have been present during a session of excessive force. I had my ears wide open to the rumor mill because I fell into the witness category.

Vic Kalama was an atypical Border Patrol Agent in several respects. Vic was an indigenous Hawaiian of Polynesian descent. Even though he had nine years with the agency, Vic was a self-proclaimed "outsider" who had no love for the "good ol' boy" network at the station. Vic was attending law school and had made connections with several Assistant U.S. Attorney's in the Southern District of California in San Diego. Vic seemed to take great pleasure in furthering the undercover investigation rumor whenever he could. I believed he was just making things up on the fly, but he was getting his desired frantic reaction by saying that his sources in San Diego told him that people from the station were going to jail.

Vic didn't seem to like anyone at the station, and it was no surprise that no one seemed to like him. For some reason, however, Vic to a liking to me. Vic knew what I had gone through with the C&Es and the recommendation to not be retained. In Vic's mind I was an outsider like him and we shared a kindred spirit. Vic worked steady midnight shifts, and whenever I worked midnights Vic would seek me out to work with him.

During those months when the fear of the investigation had reached its zenith, I had many conversations with Vic regarding its potential consequences. Some of Vic's main antagonists were also some of the most heavy-handed agents, and Vic rejoiced at the prospect of his enemies going to jail. I tried to ruin Vic's gleeful demeanor by reminding him that there were many other agents who could get hurt by this investigation, including myself.

I don't know why I decided to open up to a guy like Vic – but I did. I told Vic that I was not worried about being ID's as an abuser, because I had never laid an unnecessary hand on any detainee. I did admit, however, that I had been present when unnecessary hands were applied. I also opined that likely three quarters of the agents at San Clemente were in the same situation of having witnessed a thumping.

Vic took a momentary break from his euphoria to offer me the hope that perhaps I would be able to get out of here soon. Vic was fully aware of my desire to return east, but even with the specter of the investigation hanging over the station, I was still determined to leave under my own terms. I would either get a transfer in the federal government or another job in New York City. I was not going to just quit. Vic then threw out a statement that I never did fully understand. Vic casually mentioned that maybe the Assistant U.S. Attorney could help me get back to New York. I looked at Vic and innocently inquired why the US Attorney would want to help me. Vic just shrugged his shoulders and smiled. The only thought that came to mind was that perhaps the US attorney could arrange for me to be sent to federal prison in New York if things went bad for me.

As weeks passed, morale at the station continued to deteriorate. If there was an undercover investigation underway, it seemed that was only part of the problem. Apparently, the Southern District of California had several live complainants, including American citizens, who claimed they were beaten at the San Clemente station. The paranoia reached a fever pitch when several agents were summoned to the US attorney's office in San Diego and made to stand in a lineup for the complainants. Besides the humiliation of standing in the lineup, the agents were forced to shout vulgarities so that the complainants could also try to identify their speech patterns.

On the day of the high speed pursuit that ended with the tragic death of the Dana Point man, I did not depart the station until a little after 12:00 PM. The tragic events of the morning had me too wired to sleep, so after a stop at Carl's Jr. for my usual Superstar with cheese, I settled in on my living room sofa to watch my little black and white 17-inch television.

My eyes were rolling and my head was drooping when the phone snapped me out of my twilight state. The caller identified herself as an investigator with the Office of Professional Responsibility. Apparently, the investigator knew what had occurred on the prior shift because she commented on how fatigued I must be. She asked if she could briefly stop by my home so that I could look at a piece of paper. The investigator went on to say that this would not be a question and answer session and that I would only be interrupted for a few minutes. I told her it was alright to stop by and then went back to the sofa. You know how sometimes when you are abruptly woken from sleep, even though you are awake, it takes several minutes to really comprehend what is going on around you. I was back on the sofa for about thirty seconds when my brain began to focus. "Holy shit!" An OPR investigator was coming to my home, and I said it was OK.

At approximately 4:00 PM Mary Leonard and Joseph Conrad appeared at my door. Ms. Leonard was a very pleasant looking and sounding White female who appeared to be in her early forties. She was dressed in business attire, with blond hair that was pulled back in a bun. Her look and pleasant demeanor gave her that soccer mom next door persona. In contrast, Conrad had the look and demeanor of someone who was being terribly inconvenienced by having to be at my home. He was a balding White male in his late forties who wore a rumpled dark suit that fit well with his demeanor.

At first, Ms. Leonard did all the talking, with the conversation limited to topics like how did I like the Border Patrol and how did California compare to New York. Very subtlety, however, she began to shift the conversation. Finally, she inquired as to how I felt about the problem at the San Clemente station. When I claimed ignorance to any problems, Conrad had his cue to jump in. Very quickly it was obvious that his appearance was a match for his surly attitude.

"Come on, you know as well as I do about the beatings going on at San Clemente."

I think I managed to piss him off with the officiousness of my response. "Sir, to the best of my knowledge I do not recall witnessing anything like that."

Conrad opened a new line of questioning. "What is the procedure for handling a false claim?"

I began to talk about questions that could be used to expose a false claim when Conrad interrupted me in mid-sentence.

"Oh, come on now. Everyone knows how false claims are broken in San Clemente."

Conrad put his hands out in front of his chest, simulating grabbing someone by the collar. "It's hey carbon, and BOOM!"

He threw his hands forward as if he were slamming someone against a wall. It occurred to me that this is how a false claim must feel. It actually crossed my mind for a moment that there was a chance that this guy might really throw me against the wall of my own living room. The assault continued to be exclusively verbal, but I didn't break. Ms. Leonard dropped her soccer mom personality and joined in the fray.

"You mean to tell me that in almost two years at San Clemente, you have never seen anyone slapped, kicked, punched, or slammed against a wall."

When I stood my ground with continued denials, she threw her hands up in exasperation and said, "This is just unbelievable."

I could see how visibly upset she was becoming and I knew that wasn't good. I tried to calm things down. "I'm sorry ma'am, but I don't recall ever seeing any of these things you're bringing up."

Ms. Leonard stared at me solemnly for a long moment, and then reached into her pocketbook. She emerged with a white envelope and extended it to me. "Well, you better start recalling when you're under oath."

I opened the envelope, removed the single paper, and straightened the two folds. It was a subpoena to appear before the Grand Jury in the Southern District of California in three days. I was numb. I don't remember the investigators leaving, or if they said anything else before departing. When I emerged from my brief trance I reached for the phone and began to dial New York. Before completing the number I slammed the phone down. A call home would do no good. What was I going to tell my parents?

"Hi mom and dad – just wanted to say hi. Oh, by the way, I have to testify before a federal grand jury and there's a chance I may go to jail. Bye."

I also thought about abandoning my plan to exit on my own terms and to get out of Dodge immediately. It took about five seconds to realize that plan would never work. The long arm of the Feds would just come get me in NYC. I was just going to have to face the music at the Grand Jury.

Back at the station, rumor control was on overdrive. It had been widely held that a grand jury was being convened to look into abuses at San Clemente, but I was the first agent subpoenaed to testify. Why me? I could sense the whispers and mistrust from the good ol' boy network regarding why I had been called and what I might say.

I was directed to report to the grand jury in business attire. I did not have a suit with me so I wore a white dress shirt, blue tie, and black trousers. I had received a call from a man named Larry Barnett, who stated that he was my union attorney, and that I should meet him in a coffee shop near the court house.

He introduced himself as Larry Barnett, but I saw Cal Worthington. Anyone who has spent any time in Southern California since 1950 needs no further explanation. For those other unfortunates, Cal Worthington was the ultimate fast talking, phony smiling, corn ball used car salesman. The entire time I was in California, I could not turn on the television and go five minutes without seeing a commercial with Cal and his dog spot. The goofy routine revolved around the fact that spot was not a dog. Cal would come out riding a horse, and elephant, even a hippopotamus

As I shook hands with my new attorney, I glanced out the coffee shop window to see if any hippos were parked at the curb. Larry took a fresh legal pad out of his briefcase and prepared to make notes. I think I detected an air of disappointment when I told him that I had never touched anyone. When he asked if I had ever seen anything that may be considered abuse, I hesitated. I was shaking my head and fumbling my words. "Well, yeah. I've seen a few things, but I have no intention of saying anything."

Larry finished some notes, clicked his pen closed and placed it on top of his pad. "That's fine. But just remember something. You are the first agent being called here. Almost every agent at San Clemente will likely testify."

 I was becoming a bit irritated because I was beginning to feel as if Larry was being accusatory. "I just told you Larry, I never did anything!"

"That's not what I'm talking about. Suppose several agents place you in a room where something was happening, then what?"

I took a deep breath and bit my lip. Larry picked up his pen and pointed it at me like a teacher who had just caught a student cheating on a test. "Then, my friend. You'll have a big problem."

An uncomfortable silence ensued until I asked the logical question. "So what do I do?"

Larry waved his finger like he had just had a brain storm. "We'll get you immunity. That's what we'll do."

Immunity sounded good, I guess. But how was that going to happen?

I was pretty sure my nervousness was coming through loud and clear. This was the first time I had testified in any court proceeding, and this certainly was not what I would consider a positive appearance.

Grand juries -- first recognized in the Magna Carta, the English legal charter, in 1215 -- have been around for centuries. But their procedures are unfamiliar to most people outside the legal system. The concept of the grand jury was so firmly established in the law that the Founding Fathers provided for grand juries in the Bill of Rights. The Fifth Amendment says that "no person shall be held to answer for a capital, or otherwise infamous crime, unless on a presentment or indictment of a grand jury..."

There are several reasons why grand jury proceedings are a mystery. Witnesses appearing before a grand jury have a right to an attorney, but the lawyer must stay outside the room. The evidence is presented to the grand jurors by the prosecuting attorney, but a judge is not present. So there's no one to raise an objection -- or to consider it.

Like trial juries, grand jury deliberations are conducted in secret. Only the grand jury, the prosecutor, the witness under examination, the court reporter and an interpreter (if one is required) may be present in the grand jury room. But unlike a trial jury, a grand jury does not determine guilt or innocence -- only whether there's probable cause to believe a person or persons committed a crime. Whereas a trial jury reaches a verdict on whether the accused is convicted or acquitted, a grand jury can decide whether to bring charges via a written indictment.

The federal grand jury hears evidence presented by a federal prosecutor. The grand jury has no investigative staff of its own, so it relies on the prosecutor's information and expertise. The prosecutor shapes the case before the grand jury, deciding which witnesses will be called and what evidence to present. The grand jury may ask to call additional witnesses if necessary. It is customary for the prosecutor to question a witness first, followed by a grand jury foreperson. Then, other members of the grand jury may question the witness. Often the jurors will ask the prosecutor to ask a question, rather than asking themselves.

Federal grand juries are composed of 16 to 23 individuals selected at random "from a fair cross section of the community" in the district in which the grand jury convenes, according to the Federal Grand Jury Handbook. The names are generally drawn from lists of registered voters. Twelve of the minimum 16 members required to be present must vote in favor of an indictment before it can be returned. A witness may ask to leave the room to speak with their attorney but the lawyer is at a disadvantage, having not heard the proceedings. A witness may also invoke the Fifth Amendment privilege against self-incrimination and refuse to answer a question.

I was not enthusiastic about Larry's plan, but he was my attorney and he was looking out for my best interests, wasn't he?

Andrew Stevens paced back and forth between the grand jurors and the witness stand like he was a man on a mission. With his custom suit, perfectly coiffed hair, and confident gait. I half expected to hear the Bee Gees singing Staying Alive followed by Stevens leading the grand jurors in the hustle. The debonair AUSA stopped in front of me, with his left hand in his pants pocket and his right hand holding a legal pad.

"Would you state your name, sir?"
"Robert L. Bryan."
"And what is your current occupation Mr. Bryan?"

Time to initiate Larry's ingenious plan

"I respectfully refuse to answer that question because I truly believe the answer may incriminate me."

Stevens stood before me with his mouth wide open. I couldn't help but notice that most of the grand jurors wore similar expressions. I did not envision how slimy I would feel saying these words. Larry's great plan was for me to invoke my Fifth Amendment rights after stating my name. Larry said that after I took the fifth, he would get the AUSA to offer me immunity, and then I would return and answer questions. Larry stated that the beauty of his plan was that if somewhere down the road, testimony from other agents placed me in a compromising position, the immunity I was granted would take me off the hook.

I was thankful for the recess, if only to put a halt to my self-incrimination speech. Larry and I were taken to a small conference room adjacent to the grand jury room. When Andrew Stevens entered the room, he had the look of a man who had just been served his favorite steak. His mouth was watering. Larry explained the desire for immunity and Stevens quickly acquiesced. At that point he must really have imagined that I had a fantastic story to tell.

Soon, I was back on the witness stand. Andrew Stevens savored the wonderful aroma of that prime rib and then jabbed a tender piece with his fork and put it to his mouth. The delicious looking piece of meat turned out to be rotten, and Stevens had a sickened look on his face. The steak may have been a metaphor, but the sickened look was real. Every time I calmly stated that I never saw anything abusive at San Clemente, Steven's face took on new level of illness. Oh well, I had my immunity. Thanks Larry. Great plan! Except for one small detail. There was no immunity for perjury.

The day after my humiliating appearance at the grand jury, instead of keeping my mouth shut, I was venting about the whole experience to Joe Medina.

As I related my sad story, I detected a strange look on Joe's face. The kind of look that expresses scorn and sympathy at the same time – like telling an older kid that there is no Santa Claus.

"Hey stunod! I don't know how to tell you this but there is no immunity for perjury."

What? The whole reason for putting myself through that degrading spectacle in front of the grand jury was for the immunity. In the unlikely event that I did get jammed up in the future, it would undoubtedly be because other testifying agents placed me in situations I had already denied being in. In other words – perjury. What kind of an imbecile was Larry? At the time I was invoking my Constitutional rights, I did not realize that Larry would be better suited on top of a hippo.

One postscript on my day at the grand jury. After agreeing to immunity, Stevens had to notify the US

Marshall to bring the grand jurors back from a break. Stevens, Larry and I had two or three minutes in the conference room waiting for the jurors to get seated. In what I thought was just an attempt at social small talk, Stevens stated, "So, you miss New York, huh?"

I told him that I did, and he responded, "Well, maybe you'll get back there soon."

That was the entire conversation. The Marshal notified that the jurors were ready and Stevens prepared for the first big bite of his steak – a steak that turned out to be rotten.

Maybe I was just being infected by the paranoia running rampant at the station, but the more I thought about that brief conference room conversation with Andrew Stevens, the less I liked it. How did he know I wanted to go back to New York? As days went by more pieces of this puzzle began to fit. Why did I receive a visit from the OPR investigators? Why was I the first agent subpoenaed to the grand jury? Why did Stevens make his New York comment? The common denominator was Vic Kamala.

Vic knew about my desire to transfer to New York, and I had also admitted to Vic that I had witnessed some questionable uses of force at the station. Furthermore, Vic had several connections at the US Attorney's Office and had made the off the cuff remark about the US Attorney helping me get back to New York. Was it that farfetched to think that Vic had told Stevens that I would be an excellent cooperating witness in exchange for a transfer within the government to New York? I never found out if my theory was correct because in my remaining time at San Clemente, I never spoke to Vic again. I never confronted him, I simply avoided contact. Even if my theory was correct, my desire to return to New York was not so great that I would have become a cooperating government witness. I was very young, and in many ways stunod – but I wasn't insane. Even with my very limited experience in life I knew what being labelled a "Rat" would mean. There would be no place, including New York, where that label would not follow me. Once again, I resolved to get back to New York under my terms – and with some degree of honor.

THE INTERVIEW

I was fast approaching the two year mark on the job, and I had settled into life at the checkpoint. I was a year removed from the episode with C&Es and the ten month exam, and I was even managing to get along with the good ol' Texas boys who tried to get rid of me a year earlier. I was, however, increasingly impatient. The drama surrounding the internal investigation along with the tragic result of the most recent high speed pursuit were weighing heavily on me. I wanted out, but with the more time I put in, the more I resolved that I would never leave without getting a transfer or another job in NYC.

The transfer route had become extremely frustrating. I applied for Immigration Inspector and Deportation Officer jobs in JFK and Newark airports. I even applied for transfer as an Immigration Inspector in Philadelphia. No luck. I applied for transfer after transfer and never even got a call expressing interest from the location with the vacancy.

My buddy Frank Monte was the unofficial resident expert on transfers. Frank's wife was a Customs Inspector in Los Angeles, and Frank's sole goal in life was to transfer to Customs. Frank's constant chatter regarding Customs had begun during the first days at the academy, and had become a running joke both at the academy and for the classmates who joined him at San Clemente. He was always being ribbed about being mistakenly sworn in by the wrong agency. For all his joking, however, Frank had a plan and he apparently knew how to work it.

Frank had lived in a suburb of Chicago, and his wife had been assigned as a Customs Inspector at O'Hare. Frank had not been able to find a path directly into Customs so he settled on the Border Patrol as a means of getting his foot into the door of the federal government. When the Border Patrol job became a reality, Frank's wife began working on her own transfer to LAX. The situation worked out almost perfectly for Frank. He completed the academy and two months at San Clemente before his wife was able to join him via transfer. Frank had even rented an apartment in Fountain Valley, which was approximately equidistant between Los Angeles and San Clemente. With his wife now safely entrenched at LAX, Frank began a methodical campaign of getting to know the Customs officials at the airport. More importantly, those Customs officials were getting to know him.

On a quiet midnight shift, I was working in secondary with Frank, expressing my frustration with getting nowhere fast with my get out of town plan. I methodically recited every transfer I had applied for and been rejected. Frank shook his head, not in sympathy, but in annoyance. "I hate to be the bearer of bad news, man, but you're going about this all wrong."

"What are you talking about?"

"You could put in for a thousand transfers to New York, and you'll never get one." Frank must have sensed my annoyance as he lightened his tone a bit.

"Don't get me wrong. It's not your fault. But just think about something. I spend almost all my spare time up at LAX shaking hands and kissing babies. Why?" Frank provided a dramatic pause before answering his rhetorical question. "Because when the vacancy occurs, and I apply for it, I don't want to be just a name on a piece of paper. I want them to know who I am. Unfortunately, you are just a name on a piece of paper -3000 miles away. And I will guarantee that there are people like me back in New York knocking on the door and getting friendly with the people making the decisions on these jobs." Another pregnant pause. "That, my friend, is just a cold fact of life. If you are staying here until you can transfer east, you better prepare for a long stay."

I didn't like what Frank was saying, but he was right. My depression was deepening. I very well may be out here for a long time.

Life is always filled with surprises. Just when it had become clear that every door to New York City was locked shut, out of the blue, a key appeared to a brand new door from a most unlikely source.

I knew the call must be important when I heard my dad's voice on the other end of the phone. To be kind, my father was thrifty, and would not be making a long distance call to California during peak weekday hours if it were not important.

"Someone from the Inspector General's office called. They want to know if you want to schedule a job interview."

"For what?"

"How the hell should I know?"

"What did you tell him?"

"I told him you weren't home?"

I took the contact information and ended the conversation. After all, the minutes were piling up. I sat on my sofa with the TV on, totally oblivious to the current program. There was only one thing on my mind. Who was this offering me a job interview? I honestly had no idea. I desperately wanted to call the number, but I did not want to say, "I'm interested in the job, but, by the way – who are you?" Approximately thirty minutes later, the light switch flipped on in my brain.

Just before I graduated college I had attended a meeting of the Criminal Justice Association. During the meeting, the moderator talked about a new executive order signed by the Mayor of New York City establishing independent Inspector Generals for every NYC government agency. The point of the lecture was that all these new agencies were going to need investigative staffs, and that these new Inspector General's offices may be fruitful avenues for employment. I took the bait with enthusiasm. I left the meeting armed with a list of contact information for all these new IG offices, and I went straight to my manual typewriter and began working on a resume. Even though I could go to the library and make copies of my resume for five cents a copy, these days of the typewriter required a unique cover letter for each resume. You could not just type one letter and keep inserting the appropriate contact information. In other words, I spent most of the entire next day typing cover letters to all the IG offices requesting consideration for an investigative position. I sent letters to the IG at the Department of Corrections, Housing, Consumer Affairs, Sanitation, Fire Department, Health Department, Health & Hospitals, and many more.

My enthusiasm for these potential jobs waned with each week that I received no response to any of my resumes. Soon, my endeavor had been totally forgotten. Could it be that now, almost two years after laboring in front of my typewriter, I was receiving a response. It made no sense, but I certainly was not going to let this opportunity pass me by. I took the key that had fallen in my lap and opened the door. In other words, I dialed the phone.

"IG"s Office." That female voice was a welcome relief. At least I knew my dad had got his information straight, and I was right about where this potential job was originating from. It was also a welcome relief to sense that Mr. Robison, the Deputy Inspector General I was conversing with, seemed intrigued by my situation. He was looking at the resume of someone with a bachelor's degree in criminal justice and no real experience. Now he was talking to a Border Patrol Agent and that seemed to fascinate him. I told Mr. Robinson that I was really interested in the position of investigator, but I had one more hurdle to jump. I would be returning to New York for a week's vacation in three weeks, so I would not be able to appear for an interview until that time. Mr. Robinson did not even pause to think about my request as he scheduled my interview for 11 AM on Tuesday of the week of my vacation.

I hung up the phone, took a deep breath and slumped on the sofa, letting all the pent up tension drain from my body. For the moment, all was right with the world. But wait a minute, which Inspector General was this? I never asked, and the receptionist and Mr. Robinson had only identified themselves as the IGs office. Was it

Corrections, Fire, Housing? All I had was the address of 51 Chambers Street and an office number. Oh well, I guess I would find out when I got there.

The only thing I knew about the Inspector General was that the offices were established to investigate fraud, corruption and waste in city government. When I emerged from the subway in downtown Manhattan on that early June morning, I was getting the uncomfortable feeling that I may be sweating through my suit jacket. New York City was in the middle of a pre-summer heat wave and the temperature was approaching 90 degrees in the late morning. I was certainly no stranger to 90 plus temperatures, but this was that humid, sticky, uncomfortable New York City heat. I chuckled as I scanned addresses on Chambers Street. To think, I wanted to come back to this.

Built in 1912, 51 Chambers Street was a very ornate 17-story building that was the original home to the Emigrant Industrial Savings Bank, but was presently serving as the home to many New York City government agencies. The elevator was likely the original from 1912. It was going to take a while to reach the 12th floor as the car rose upward at its snail's pace. As my elevator ride neared completion, I removed a paper from my pants pocket to confirm my destination – room 1201.

The elevator door opened and there, very conveniently, directly in front of me was 1201. I was stunned. It wasn't the office number that stunned me, it was the printing on the door directly below that did the trick – DEPARTMENT OF SANITATION. Department of Sanitation? What kind of corruption was taking place with garbage?

From my perspective, the interview went remarkably well. But remember, other than the oral exam for the Border Patrol, I had no real experience in an interview setting. Nothing less than being physically thrown out of the building would have convinced me the interview did not go well.

I learned that there were many corruption issues involved with garbage. There were cases involving trade waste, where merchants who should be contracting private carters were actually paying off sanitation workers to remove their trash. There were also numerous cases of payoffs involving snow plowing private parking lots and driveways, as well as many instances of sanitation workers abusing their generous sick leave.

It all seemed very interesting and I wanted to learn more. Mr. Robinson, however, was much more focused on learning about life as a Border Patrol Agent. I guess his interest was a good thing, and I left that interview feeling very good about my chances of getting the job. As usual, however, I failed to address some basic issues, the most basic of which was when they planned on filling the position. On the subway back to Queens, I envisioned a fantasy where I would receive a job offer by Friday, while I was still in New York. That fantasy seemed unlikely. As my train crossed under the East River I faced the reality that it had taken almost two years to get an interview. How long was it going to take to fill the position? Oh well, I could dream for a few days, couldn't I? Friday passed with no call and Sunday afternoon found me lifting off from JFK for my return to the checkpoint. It wasn't a good feeling.

STILL IN PURSUIT

It was another beautiful Saturday morning in late June in Southern California. I had finally stopped spending every minute of my off duty time perched next to the phone, waiting for that call from the Inspector General's office that never came.

I was working the day shift, and as I stood in the checkpoint secondary position, leaning leisurely on the pursuit vehicle, I could not help but marvel at the environment. It was about 9:30 AM and a refreshing breeze off the Pacific Ocean made the 80 degree temperature sheer perfection. I was paying little attention to the actual checkpoint, but was instead focused on the hypnotic effect of the ocean. I had spent many days at Rockaway Beach in New York City, and the waters of the Atlantic Ocean always struck me as being a rather unattractive shade of pale green. I fully realize that scientists will tell you that water, by itself, is clear but that your perception of its color can be influenced by your perspective, the state of the sunlight, the depth of the water, wave action, and probably some other factors. I am not disputing science. All I know is that the Atlantic Ocean appeared green to me while this beautiful ocean I was staring at was a deep shade of gorgeous blue.

I came out of my trance, shook my head and chuckled. There were people back east who would sell their souls to live in this environment, and I was actively trying to get out of it. It had been two weeks since the job interview in New York City and I was becoming nervous. Whether I got the job or not – I just wanted to know.

As I enjoyed the view of the Pacific, Agent Lester Fulton stood behind the checkpoint stop sign, waving vehicles forward on both sides of him. Agent Bob Remy was in secondary with me, but he was not enjoying the view. He was actually doing the right thing by focusing on what Lester was doing behind the stop sign. Bob had just graduated from the academy a month earlier, and for the first time I was in the position of being the experienced veteran. I know I should have been helpful in trying to help Bob learn the job at the checkpoint, but I had pretty much lost interest. The paranoia and rumors surrounding the seemingly never ending internal investigation, made all too real by the visit from the internal investigators and the subsequent grand jury had soured my attitude. Throw in the fact that I believed there was a potential exit strategy via my recent New York City job interview, and the result was a Border Patrol Agent who would much rather stare at the beautiful Pacific Ocean than worry about illegal aliens getting through the checkpoint. Don't get me wrong, I was not unsociable towards Bob, but at that point I just did not have the motivation to talk about doing the job.

At about 9:30 AM, my study of the ocean was interrupted by a thud and a shout. The thud was a Maglite striking the rear driver's side quarter panel of a black, 1974 Dodge Monaco. The shout was Lester's notification that the Dodge had ignored his order to stop and was now accelerating north on the freeway.

I jumped into the driver's seat of the pursuit vehicle, and when Bob slammed the passenger door shut, we were off.

The Dodge was continuing to accelerate while it weaved in and out of freeway traffic.

822 was the radio code for the San Clemente Border Patrol Station office. When we were involved in a pursuit, our radio transmissions only went to our office. If we needed the California Highway Patrol, the San Clemente PD, or any other local law enforcement agency, these requests would have to go through 822. The vehicle I was driving was 9116, so in border patrol radio protocols, the transmission began with who was being called followed by who was calling. In other words, our radio transmission would always begin with 822-9116.

Since I was driving it was Bob's role to keep 822 informed of the status of the pursuit. In a pursuit, this entailed transmitting our speed, location and direction of travel on an ongoing basis. I knew Bob had never been involved in a Border Patrol pursuit, so I instructed him to simply keep letting 822 know where we are. There was a brief moment of silence followed by Bob's inquiry, "Where are we?" We were approaching 100 mph and all I could do was laugh. This wasn't Bob's fault. He was new here. He certainly wasn't born with geographical knowledge of the area. I calmly explained, "Just tell 822 what I say."

We used landmarks on or near the freeway to note our location. For example, about a mile north of the checkpoint there was a large tree off the N/B side of the freeway. I forget the type of tree it was, but that was one of our normal landmarks. A radio transmission might indicate that a vehicle stop was being made 100 yards north of the (   ) tree. The San Onofre Nuclear Plant was another landmark as well as the first Basilone Road exit sign. After that, it was usually exits and off ramps that marked location.

I started speaking and Bob started repeating into the radio

Me: nuclear plant

Bob: 822-9116: we are northbound passing the nuclear plant

Me: Basilone Road sign

Bob: 822-9116: approaching the Basilone Road sign

And so it went on for about twelve miles, with the speed topping out at approximately 100 mph. The Dodge had been in the left lane, but abruptly crossed over all the lanes to access an off ramp.

Me: Beach Cities, Highway 1 off ramp.

Bob: Vehicle has exited at the Beach Cities, Highway 1 exit

At the top of this off ramp the road makes a drastic turn to the left, so when the Dodge made this turn, I lost visual contact for several seconds. I had to substantially slow down to maintain control into the sharp curve. Coming out of the curve, the road was straight and the view unimpeded – but the Dodge was nowhere in sight. This was impossible. There were no exits. The only place to go for the next mile was to remain on the road. As I was trying to process what could have happened, I noticed three cars stopped on the right shoulder of the road. It appeared the people in these vehicles were pointing to something beyond the shoulder of the road.

It turned out that I was wrong. There was an alternative to remaining on the road. I had not considered it at the time, but instead of remaining on the road you could go off the road in that sharp curve and plummet down a one hundred foot embankment to arrive near the intersection of Camino Capistrano and Via Cannon. That is exactly the option the Dodge had taken.

I parked 9116 on the shoulder and Bob and I slid down the embankment as quickly as possible. The Dodge was resting upright in a grassy area near the intersection with heavy smoke engulfing the vehicle. With the help of two good Samaritans, Bob and I were able to pry open the trunk. A male who appeared to be in his 60s had begun the trip locked in the trunk, but was now wedged between the trunk and the back seat. His head was sticking into the back seat area while the rest of his body was in the trunk.

He was conscious, but he was not in good shape. He had numerous deep lacerations all over his face and head, and the unnatural position of his arms and legs indicated that they were fractured. Also in the trunk was a male in his early teens who was also conscious, but with terrible looking damage to his left eye. Miraculously, a young female carrying an infant exited the front passenger seat unaided, and neither the female nor the infant appeared to be seriously injured.

Normally, we would not touch someone as severely injured as the older male. We would wait for the fire department and ambulance personnel to ply their trade. But we had no choice. With the smoke pouring out of the Dodge, we didn't know if it was about to go up in flames or explode. Again, with the help of the good Samaritans, we pulled the male out through the trunk. I can still hear his anguished screams as we freed him from his trapped condition. Soon the fire department, ambulances, and California Highway Patrol were on the scene. The older male was transported to Mission Hospital in Mission Viejo, while the teen with the severely injured eye was taken to San Clemente General Hospital. I never heard anything further about their condition.

What about the driver of that Dodge, who failed to yield at the checkpoint, took us on a dangerous high speed chase up the freeway for twelve miles and then drove off the highway severely injuring his passengers. He ran away from the scene to parts unknown. That was one arrest I really would have enjoyed making.

The next day I was back at the checkpoint, admiring the Pacific Ocean – waiting for that call that would take me home to New York City.

SALVATION

A few weeks after returning from my New York vacation / job interview, I moved into a rotation of midnight shifts. The shift rotation at San Clemente was by month, but swapping shifts for the month was authorized, as long as two agents were agreeable to the trade. The agents were divided into three squads, so in order to be able to work a steady shift an agent would have to have a "swap buddy" in the two other squads.

I noticed a significant spike in my popularity when it was discovered that I did not mind working midnights. Whenever my squad was due to rotate into a month of day tours or 4 x 12s, there was usually a line of agents waiting to corner me to see if I would swap for their month of midnights. I usually agreed, so I spent the bulk of my time during my last year at the station working midnights.

I was less than a week into a new midnight rotation and the silence from NYC was still deafening. Answering machines may have existed in 1980, but I certainly did not have one. If anyone wanted to reach me by phone they had to catch me at home. I had thought about my inability to be reached easily during the interview, so I had suggested to Mr. Robinson that he continue to use my NYC contact number if he needed to reach me.

It was about 8:30 AM when I entered my living room after an uneventful midnight shift. The sound of the phone was resonating inside the room.

My mom sounded very irritated. "Where have you been? I thought you got off work at 8 AM. I've been calling all morning."

My response reeked of sarcasm "I think I heard of this thing called a three- hour time difference, haven't you?"

Good old mom. Over a year and a half out here and she still couldn't get used to the time difference. She paid no mind to my sarcasm and pushed ahead.

"Anyway, you have to call the Inspector General's Office right away."

"What about?"

"I don't know, just call Mr. Robinson now!"

My mother was no shrinking violet. In fact, some people might say she was a bit nervy. The point is that my mom would not have fielded a call from Mr. Robinson without finding out if I had gotten the job.

The call to Mr. Robinson was merely a formality. The message from my mother was loud and clear – I had gotten the job offer. I spoke to Mr. Robinson and arranged for a start date in four weeks. I wanted to give two weeks' notice to the Border Patrol and then have two weeks of R&R before embarking on a new occupational adventure.

I was excited. Salvation was finally at hand. Once again, all was right with the world.

That night I went to work and completed another uneventful shift. I did not tell anyone about my plans. I wanted to wait to break the news to the station chief first. Chief Wallace usually came in about 9AM so I waited around for his arrival in the administrative room. Right at 9 AM he strode through the parking lot door, completely ignoring me as he headed toward his office. I followed and stood in his doorway.

"Excuse me chief, can I have a brief word."

He never moved his focus from the folders on his desktop. "What is it?"

He never invited me inside the office, so I continued the conversation from the doorway. "I'm going to resign and take a job back in New York, so I just want to know what steps I have to follow."

That statement got his attention. He still never invited me inside the office, but he rose from his desk and approached me at the doorway, hand extended. As we shook hands, he stated in that all too familiar Texas drawl, "That's a shame. You've really become an old hand around here."

All I could do was smile. That was probably the most outrageous statement I had heard in two years. The only conversation I ever had with this man was when he told me how deficient I was and handed me the C&E where he recommended that I not be retained. Now, I was an old hand. One of the good ol' boys I guess. I didn't know how to respond. Was I supposed to say "Well thanks pardner" and shout "Yahoo?" I continued to smile as the handshake broke and got back on point. "So what steps do I have to follow?"

The chief explained that I actually had to complete the resignation paperwork at the Chula Vista sector. He continued to say that on my last work day, I would report to San Clemente – take a car down to Chula Vista – complete the resignation paperwork – and return to San

Clemente. When I departed the San Clemente station that day, I would turn in my gun and shield and my career with the United States Border Patrol would be over.

Two weeks flew by, and when I arrived at Chula Vista, I was directed to a supervisory agent who I had never seen before. He gave me all the resignation paperwork and began going over it with me. When we came to part III, the supervisor explained that I needed to write out my reasons for resigning, and that I needed to be specific. He emphasized that I should avoid general terms such as "personal reasons". This was going to be problematic because I had already determined that "personal reasons" was going to be the full extent of my statement.

The resignation paperwork provided a full page to articulate the reasons for leaving the agency. With the form safely in front of me, the supervisor left the room, hesitating momentarily for a parting comment.

"Take your time. I'll be back in a few minutes."

With pen in hand, I got right to work. The form began with a pre-printed "I resign for the following reasons." Even with the fresh directions from the supervisor I printed boldly PERSONAL REASONS, and put the pen down on the table. I was done.

Ten minutes later the supervisor returned. He collected the paperwork and began his review. When he came to part III, he didn't say a word. He stood up and began to leave the room, voicing a very irritated "Wait here." Before he departed.

Five minutes later the door opened and in walked a uniformed chief. I'd seen this chief before, but I was having difficulty remembering where. I was mildly surprised by his pleasant smile as he sat across the table from me. "Hi Bob, I'm Chief Gardner."

With the sound of his voice and the recognition of his name, I instantly recalled my association with this man. A little over a year earlier, Chief Gardner was the one who passed me through the ten month exam when I had just about come to the realization that all hope was lost. Obviously, the chief had reviewed the paperwork before entering the room, accounting for the knowledge of my first name and accompanying informal salutation.

"I wanted to have a quick word with you about your resignation statement."

I was beginning to feel a bit guilty and a bit agitated at the same time.

"I'm sorry chief, I don't want to cause any problems. I just want to get this over with and go home."

"I know, I know," the chief responded empathetically, but you could really do us a favor with this resignation.

"I don't understand"

"Some of the stuff that has gone on during this internal investigation has been outrageous, and I know you know it because you have been subject to some of the nonsense."

Chief Gardner leaned forward. "If you went on record with the fact that this investigation was at least in part the reason for your resignation, you'd be doing us all a great service."

I was shaking my head and my mouth was open, but no words were coming out. I really did not want to do this. I had made many mistakes over the past two years and I certainly did not want to make another. I envisioned a long career in law enforcement ahead of me, and I did not want to memorialize the fact that I was chased out of the Border Patrol because of my fear of an internal investigation. Still, I owed this man big time. Maybe he simply hadn't read my file closely and seen all the negative C&Es. Maybe he had a beef with the chief of the San Clemente station and thought he would stick it to him by passing me. Whatever the reason, when all appeared lost, Chief Gardner gave me a fair deal.

"OK chief, let me have a blank form."

This wasn't just a new opportunity for me to express myself. This time, the chief looked over my shoulder and collaborated for the next fifteen minutes until the statement was just right. When I put my pen down again, I had composed the following statement:

I have been offered employment with the New York City Inspector General's Office. I believe job opportunities with that department are better than with the US Border Patrol at this time. I am influenced in my decision by the internal investigation now being conducted at the San Clemente station. A copy of my memo from May 14, 1980 is attached and accurately portrays what I consider to be a complete lack of respect and courtesy to an officer of the Immigration and Naturalization Service. Other incidents, such as the use of investigatory lineups accompanied by commands to shout vulgar epithets have been humiliating and degrading. I view the increase in investigators assigned to internal investigations as a purposeful witch hunt politically motivated in an election year. I feel completely insecure in my position. I feel I am denied counselling by my chief and other supervisors who claim they are as ignorant of the scope of the internal investigation as I am. The job situation at San Clemente is highly stressful and I believe I will be able to serve better in a more understanding and appreciative environment. According to the investigators, I am not a target of the current investigation at San Clemente. I have enjoyed my work in the Border Patrol and my associations. I am sincerely sad to leave the Border Patrol which I joined with such high aspirations.

Chief Gardner read the statement thoughtfully, despite the fact that he had dictated most of it.

He extended his hand. "Thanks much son. You're doing the right thing for us."

As I drove north on the freeway I had mixed feelings about what had just transpired. I feared that somewhere down the road when I least expected it, this resignation statement would come back to bite me. Basically, the statement was documenting that I left the Border Patrol because I could not deal with the stress of an internal investigation into brutality and violations of civil rights. Not exactly a selling point to highlight to other law enforcement agencies considering hiring me. This uneasy feeling stayed with me all the way back to San Clemente and through the submittal of my gun and shield to the supervisor on duty.

When I pulled my Firebird out of the parking lot, I had reached a degree of peace with the resignation statement. I still wasn't happy with what I had written, but I believed there was a greater issue. I had shown loyalty to someone who was there for me at my lowest point. In my final act as a Border Patrol Agent, I hoped I had shown Chief Gardner that I was someone he could ride the river with.

HOME

My career conducting garbage investigations with the Inspector General's Office was short lived. Approximately three months after returning to New York City a civil service exam was given for Transit Police Officer. Within a year my career as a police officer in New York City had begun.

Twenty years later the ride was over. I had progressed from police officer to captain, working a wide range of assignments, including patrol, academy instructor, internal affairs, and narcotics. My career also involved an involuntary department change thanks to the New York City police merger in 1995.

Prior to 1995, New York City was policed by three separate police departments – the New York City Police Department, the NYC Transit Police Department, and the NYC Housing Police Department. With the police merger, the Transit and Housing departments ceased to exist and I became a member of the NYPD.

SHAMELESS PROMOTION ALERT: My experiences throughout my NYC police career are chronicled in the original DARK KNIGHTS.

My time in the Border Patrol was brief, but it made a lasting impression on me. I remained in contact with only two people from my Border Patrol days. I communicated with Rick Sanders frequently for the first couple of years after I returned to New York. Rick was my source for updates on the internal investigation. Unfortunately, the situation had only gotten worse, culminating in the arrest of three members of the San Clemente station – a supervisor and two agents.

Rick sent me all the newspaper articles at the time, and it turned out that some of the rumors had been right. The Office of Professional Responsibility had in fact sent in undercover agents posing as illegal aliens, and these undercovers had been the victims of unnecessary force.

Reading the stories about these arrests made me very happy to be three thousand miles away.

Rick resigned about six months after me and moved his family to his original home – Oklahoma. Rick became a police officer in Broken Arrow, a suburb of Tulsa. Shortly after Rick made his move I visited him in Broken Arrow. There just happened to be a police officer test being given during the week I was visiting, and he convinced me to take the test and the subsequent interview. About a month after the visit I received a call from the Chief of the Broken Arrow Police Department offering me a police officer position. I had learned many things from my Border Patrol experience, but by far the most important factor I learned about myself was that for better or worse, I was a New Yorker. I declined the position.

I lost track of Rick many years ago. This break in communications was not by design and there had been no falling out between Rick and me. This was simply an example of one of my many flaws. Without intending any offense, I just find it very easy to cease communications with people after they are no longer a part of my day to day life. I have done this with childhood friends, college friends, and I am now going through this with a number of good friends I made during my police career.

Amazingly, I found that technology could make up for my character flaw. I recently received a Facebook message from Rick's wife, and as a result, Rick and I are in communication again after all these years.

Steve Caridi also resigned from the Border Patrol within a year of me. Steve returned to the Bronx and became a cop in Westchester County. I maintained fairly regular contact with Steve, and actually got together once for a beer. As was my norm, however, for no particular reason the communication stopped.

My re-engagement with Rick inspired me to try to open up the communication lines with Steve. Unfortunately, he did not appear to be using social media. I did find some references to him on the Internet, however. Steve had completed his entire career in Westchester County, retiring at the rank of lieutenant. I found an online article reflecting that Steve was suing the county for something that wasn't totally clear in the article. Maybe it was something as egregious as having to put a small (t) after his name.

Wait a minute! The story is not complete. Some of you having been hanging in from the A&S department store chapter, waiting for the promised ironic twist. Well, here it is.

EPILOGUE: THE IRONIC TWIST

Queens, New York City: 2007

I've always hated going to social events alone, and this night was no different. I muttered a couple of choice words under my breath and put my cell phone back in its holder. All the calls had gone right to Kevin's voicemail. I stood alone in the dimly lit railroad parking lot pondering my next move. It was now thirty minutes past the time Kevin was due to arrive on the Long Island Railroad. After all these years and the numerous missed appointments, you'd think I would have learned my lesson. I tapped my fingers on the hood of my car, keeping the beat to some distant music. The sounds flowed across the parking lot from the only local source of light - the brightly illuminated front entrance of the Black Oak Pub. When would I learn? I had known Kevin for over thirty years and nothing had changed. He was as unreliable today as he was when we worked as store detectives in Abraham & Strauss so many years ago.

Kevin was my only link to those days, but it wasn't much of a connection as Kevin had not talked to anyone from A&S in over twenty years. Then came social media. In 2007 Facebook was just something I heard my kids talking about, but Kevin was in deep. So it was with a high degree of interest and curiosity that I listened to Kevin describe a group he had discovered on Facebook. He said that the group was for people who had worked at the defunct A&S department store, and that a reunion was being organized at a pub near the Mineola LIRR station for those who had worked in the Queens Center store.

I paced around my car considering my next move. Kevin was a no show, leaving me with two choices. I could walk into the pub alone, seeking out people who I had not seen in over thirty years, or I could get back in my car and go home. Slowly, I drifted toward the music and the lights. The tempting smell of burgers made it easier to continue. I took one last deep breath before pulling open the heavy wooden door and entering the pub.

The interior was dark, and the heavy black beams running the length of the ceiling signaled that the pub was very old. From what I could make out in the dimly lit conditions, framed photographs of hockey players covered the walls, along with a motley assortment of what appeared to be very old Long Island fishing and aviation paraphernalia. There were also several hand-painted wood signs in Gaelic that I had no interest in reading, and even less interest in trying to pronounce.

The pub reeked atmosphere, but it was also jammed - more jammed than even my social awkwardness had feared. The music, which had served as a distant background in the parking lot, was now pulsating in my head. My countdown to an about face and exit had reached T-minus three seconds when it was put on hold.

"You here for the A&S reunion? They're in the back."

I had absolutely no idea who this affable fellow was with his hand on my shoulder, guiding me through the throng at the bar. Oh well. 3-2-1- blast off. There was no turning back now.

I was guided to a table in the back of the pub where my guide picked up a blank sticker.

"What years did you work at the store?"

My response prompted him to take a blue sharpie and write 1975-77 on the sticker. He then pulled off the protective paper and affixed the sticker to my jacket. This man had a similar sticker attached, only his read 1987-94. Hmm, I was seeing the set-up. Not a bad idea. The A&S store in Queens Center was open from 1973 - 1995. Time frame would be more important than names, so the organizers set up a system where people could scan the pub to identify people who had worked in the store at the same time, and let them handle the introductions from there.

I wedged my way to the bar and finally got one of the bartender's attention for a Bud Light. I was able to establish ownership of a small piece of real estate at the end of the bar. This is where I set up camp, scanning stickers for anyone who I may have worked with.

I was in the middle of my third beer, and I had seen no one with a sticker with my period of employment. This was a big waste of time. A short, chunky guy wedged his way into my real estate. Although annoyed, I did my best to create a comfortable position even though this interloper was now pressing up against my left side. He didn't say excuse me or acknowledge me at all. He was intent on ordering a scotch and soda. Once he had his drink, he managed to turn his body in my direction.

"You one of the A&S Guys?" he commented in recognition of the sticker.

I nodded in between sips of beer. He must have noticed my visual scan of his clothing.

"I'm not putting that stupid sticker on." With his free hand he pointed at my sticker. "Hey we must have worked together."

I was suddenly interested. I put my bottle on the bar. "What's your name?" My hand was extending as best as possible in the tight quarters as I asked the question.

"Juan Morales. Who are you Cheech?"

If that didn't put a proper exclamation point on my night. I make one connection and it ends up being with the person I wanted to connect with the least. This was the obnoxious guy who I was convinced was either a thief or an undercover agent. Even though it was over thirty years ago, I also hadn't forgotten how this guy tried to steal my leather jacket shoplifting case. The Juan Morales I had worked with in 1976-77 was short, rail thin, with a bushy afro hairstyle. This version was still short, but was significantly overweight and completely bald. At least I had something to feel good about on this wasted evening.

"So what have you been up to Cheech?"

We went through the mandatory small talk for a few minutes. I was trying to be polite and not show my complete disinterest in learning that Juan had recently retired from the Washington DC Metropolitan Police, and had now returned to New York City.

My fourth beer removed my filters, so I asked the only question about Juan Morales that interested me.

"When you worked at the store, I figured you were either a thief or an undercover. Which was it?"

Juan sipped his drink and smiled. I thought I would receive a smart ass answer to my smart ass question, but instead, his answer was direct and to the point

"Undercover."

I don't know why I was stunned. This answer verified one of my theories, but still, there was a degree of amazement.

I followed up. "Did you ever catch anyone? You were still there after I left in 77."

"No Cheech, it was all bullshit. Federated Department Stores must have got all paranoid when that guy on overnights got caught filling up his car on the loading dock, so they sent me in."

The Budweiser was prompting me to continue with the smartass approach.

"So, your undercover career was a complete bust, huh?"

I was obviously failing to strike any nerve, as Juan's response was calm and measured. "I guess you could say that Cheech. But that was all penny ante bullshit anyway. I got into some real heavy undercover shit a few years later."

I guess I was interested in hearing his story, and out of bar room etiquette, the next time the bartender cruised by,

I signaled for another beer plus a scotch and soda for Juan. Juan raised his glass in salute.

"Thanks Cheech."

With the obligatory gratitude completed, he was off and running with his story.

"In 1979 I got a job as a Detention Officer with US Immigration. It was mostly a bullshit job, as all I did was drive a detention bus around the Tri-State area, transporting illegal aliens from one federal detention facility to another. I was about ready to pack it in with the job when my supervisor told me that the Office of Professional Responsibility was looking for Spanish speaking Hispanic males for a big undercover operation on the west coast. I applied and OPR scooped me up and sent me out west."

"What were you actually doing?"

"OPR had opened a big investigation into reports of the Border Patrol beating on the illegal aliens."

My eyes widened as I nearly dropped my bottle. "Was your operation in San Clemente?"

Now it was Juan's eyes that widened. "Yeah, how do you know about San Clemente?"

"I was a Border Patrol Agent there. When was your operation?"

"1980"

"Oh my God. I was there in 1980."

We both were at a loss for words. We looked away from each other and sipped our drinks. I turned back towards him. No more smartass questions. I really wanted to know the story.

"So what happened?"

Juan Morales and a partner were set up in the undercover role of illegal aliens, with the intent of being apprehended by agents at the San Clemente station. Sometime during the spring of 1980 Juan and his partner boarded a northbound Greyhound bus at Oceanside. Their OPR handlers had dressed them in traditional Mexican garb, complete with serapes, and huaraches, the traditional Mexican sandal. Even Juan admitted that the get up was ridiculous with the only preposterous accessory missing being a sombrero. To add another degree of realism, they were told not to shower or wash their hair for three days, and their clothes were given to them already covered with a layer of dirt.

The bus stopped outside the San Clemente station and the driver disappeared inside the station door. Thirty seconds later the same door swung open and Agent Les Fulton emerged. Les boarded the Greyhound and made a pleasant announcement from the front that he was conducting an immigration inspection. As Les approached Juan and his partner in the middle of the bus, they went into their very simple illegal alien act. In other words, they sat silently with wide eyes, staring straight ahead, not acknowledging his presence. A minute later they were standing inside a prisoner processing room being frisked by Les Fulton.

By OPR's design, the frisk uncovered fraudulent I-151s possessed by both detainees. Juan explained that these Green Cards were bad fakes, obvious enough that even a novice agent would recognize the lack of authenticity. Les brought the partner to a holding cell and then returned to the processing room with Juan. Juan said that Les was professional and unemotional as he began typing the apprehension paperwork. Les left both fake green cards out on the table next to the typewriter. Les asked him where he had obtained the green card, and as scripted, Juan said that he didn't know. The answer did not seem to have any impact on Les, as he simply kept typing.

Juan did not recall Less Fulton calling for any assistance, but about five minutes after he began typing, Agent Joe Barton entered the processing room. This was the same Joe Barton with the hair trigger temper who almost got me strung up as a human piñata. Joe walked directly to the table and picked up the fake green cards. Holding both cards in one hand, Joe turned toward Juan and asked where he had obtained them. Juan stayed on script by shrugging his shoulders and muttering a very meek "No se, senor."

Joe calmly placed the green cards back on the table, and in one fluid motion drove both his hands into Juan's shoulders with great force, driving Juan into the cinder block office wall. Juan remained upright but the impact with the wall had knocked the wind out of him. Joe re-engaged, placing his face about two-inches from Juan's, asking him if the experience had jarred his memory. Juan didn't answer, but this time it was not by design. He was beginning to panic.

Even though brutality was the major focus of the investigation, his OPR handlers had not provided a safety plan regarding how to extricate himself if he started taking a serious beating. As he stood with his body still vibrating from its sudden trip to the wall, Juan was considering identifying himself as a government undercover agent.

That thought only served to increase his sense of panic with the realization that such an admission may be the trigger to get himself killed. Juan resolved that there was nothing he could do but take it.

He endured three more trips to the wall at the hands of Joe Barton. Juan believed he had reached the end of the line when Joe picked up a chair, held it over his head and threatened to cave in Juan's head. Juan closed his eyes and tensed his body in anticipation of impact. No impact came, and instead Barton left the room without comment.

Juan was breathing heavily and Les Fulton asked if he was alright. Les had done nothing to assist Joe's attack, but he had done nothing to stop it either. The break in the action was short lived, as Joe Barton returned with Supervisory Agent Jack Worth. Worth went right for the green card - held the card a couple of inches from Juan's face - and asked who gave it to him. Juan said nothing - this time solely out of fear upon noticing that Worth was carrying a very large flashlight in his right hand.

Worth asked the question again and Juan remained silent. The next thing Juan remembered was being doubled over in pain, the result of a flashlight thrust into his stomach. Les Fulton assisted him to the holding cell and he spent the next several hours lying on the hard wooden bench trying to gain his composure. At some point, Juan remembered his partner being placed into the holding cell in much the same condition as him.

It was early in the pre-dawn hours of the next morning that the immigration bus brought them to the San Ysidro port of entry. Juan and his partner went through the turnstiles into Tijuana. They were approached by one of his OPR handlers who excitedly asked how things went. Juan said his simple answer to the handler was "Fuck you!"

I was a powder keg of conflicting emotions. Excitement, fear, sadness, rage, and wonder were vying for possession of my consciousness. It had been 27-years since San Clemente and all the memories were rushing back. There was no way for me to determine where I was when Juan was taking his beating. Most likely, I was off duty or working a different shift.

What would have happened if I had walked into the station and recognized Juan after he had received his thumping? A more sobering thought was the fact that I had been present for several sessions similar to Juan's and just like Les Fulton, I had not participated, but I had also done nothing to stop it. I certainly never reported the incidents and actually denied seeing anything to the OPR investigators and at the grand jury. What if any of the incidents I witnessed had involved undercover agents. I may have ended up sharing a cell with Les Fulton.

I felt bad for all three of my former colleagues. I enjoyed working with Joe Barton and Jack Worth was a top-notch supervisor. Based on my experiences with them, however, I believed every word of Juan's story. In conducting further Internet research, I learned that Jack Worth had also plead guilty to thumping a U.S. citizen and then shipping this American to Mexico via the Tijuana turnstiles. My real sympathy was reserved for Les Fulton.

Les had maintained his personal professionalism, but failed to report the abuse, and then denied witnessing it – just like I did. The only difference between Les and me was that undercover agent Juan Morales was the victim of the abuse Les denied witnessing – a denial that led straight to a perjury charge.

When I shook hands and parted company with Juan Morales, I was conflicted. Unexpectedly, a time portal had been opened to a time 27-years earlier. I still didn't like Juan, but that had nothing to do with San Clemente. Ultimately, he was still the same obnoxious, nervy jerk from 27-year earlier.

Come on, you have to agree that I wasn't kidding when I urged you to keep reading for the ironic twist. What are the odds that a guy I worked with in a college job would end up being the catalyst for sending several Border Patrol agents from my station to jail, and how astronomical do those odds get that I would find out about his undercover role in a chance meeting 27-years later. I told you to keep reading, didn't I?

Made in the USA
Columbia, SC
09 March 2021